Business Communication

Topics & Activities

Fourth Edition

Richard D. Featheringham

Nancy Hicks

Kendall Hunt
publishing company

Cover image © Shuttestock, Inc.

Kendall Hunt
publishing company

www.kendallhunt.com
Send all inquiries to:
4050 Westmark Drive
Dubuque, IA 52004-1840

ABOUT THE AUTHORS

Dr. Richard D. Featheringham is a Professor Emeritus at Central Michigan University where he taught courses in business communication, business report writing, advanced composition, and business ethics for the College of Business Administration for over 36 years.

Dr. Featheringham has given presentations on the national and international levels and has researched, written and consulted extensively in the areas of national and international business communication, business ethics, business information systems, and teaching methodology.

Dr. Featheringham received the Excellence in Teaching Award from Central Michigan University, the College of Business Administration (CMU) Dean's Teaching Award (twice), the College of Business (CMU) Ameritech Excellence in Teaching Award, the Outstanding Educator of the Year Award from the National Court Reporters Association, the Outstanding Teaching Excellence Award from the Academy of Business Administration, the Mortar Board Outstanding Faculty of the Year award, and was selected several times for the Who's Who Among America's Teachers award.

Dr. Featheringham served as faculty advisor to Alpha Kappa Psi, the professional business fraternity, for over 35 years. Dr. Featheringham continues to consult in the area of business communications.

Dr. Nancy Hicks is a Professor in the Business Information Systems Department at Central Michigan University, Mount Pleasant, Michigan. She received her Ph.D. from Michigan State University in 1994. Dr. Hicks has been teaching for over 20 years at the post-secondary level. She teaches several business communication courses in the Applied Business Practices minor program including Applied Business Communication and Business Practices, Communication, and Collaboration. Dr. Hicks also serves as a faculty adviser for the Applied Business Practices program.

Dr. Hicks focuses her research on issues related to communication skills, pedagogy, and how students learn. She participates in conferences at the state, national, and international levels. She also conducts workshops for employers, students, and professional organizations on a variety of topics including effective communication, written and oral communication skills, effective presentations and presentation skills, and innovative teaching strategies.

Dr. Hicks has received numerous teaching awards including the Excellence in Teaching Award from CMU, the College of Business Administration (CMU) Dean's Teaching Award, the College of Business (CMU) Ameritech Excellence in Teaching Award, the Outstanding Post-secondary Teacher of the Year Award from the Michigan Business Education Association, and has been selected several times for Who's Who Among America's Teachers.

CONTENTS

UNIT III—WRITTEN COMMUNICATION continued	Page

Unit I - Employment Communication

Capstone Project for Unit I - Employment Communication

The Capstone Project for Unit I is designed to apply the main topics in this unit into one integrated assignment. The integration of the unit topics via the completed assignments will result in an employment resource portfolio that will consist of the following:

1. Two versions of your current résumé (in chronological and scannable formats)

2. Solicited cover letter for an internship or a job

3. Unsolicited cover letter for an internship or a job

4. Thank-you letter for an interview

5. A letter of recommendation

6. Letter accepting a position

7. Letter rejecting a position

8. A follow-up letter for an application

9. A two-sided business card

10. Common interview questions with answers. Refer to the lists at the end of this unit and outline your answers to these common interview questions as assigned by your instructor.

11. Conduct company research. Select a company to research in preparing for an interview. See pages 49-50 for the company research assignment.

TOPIC   **Résumés** (examples pages 11-17)

DEFINITION   A résumé is an employment document that summarizes relevant qualifications, skills, and experiences. A résumé should be selective focusing on the specific position you are applying for. Several types of résumés exist. The most common types are explained below. Be sure to determine which type of résumé is appropriate for the position you are applying for.

There are two common types of résumé:

1. *Chronological résumés* (actually reverse chronological) are the most common résumé format for college students. This type of résumé emphasizes education followed by work experience in reverse chronological sequence (most recent listed first).

2. *Functional résumés* are achievement oriented and emphasize skills and abilities first rather than education. Functional résumés are used when your education and work experience don't necessarily match the job qualifications and/or when someone has been out of the workforce. This résumé format utilizes skill sets that focus on relevant skills to demonstrate your qualifications. An example of a functional résumé can be found on page 17.

Other types of résumés include the following:

- *Curriculum vitaes* (also known as a CV, vita, or vitae) are an academic version of a résumé. A CV consists of a detailed list of educational achievements such as publications, presentations, professional activities, awards and honors.

- *Government résumés* are designed specifically for government positions. Résumés for government jobs differ significantly from those for private sector jobs. A government résumé has very specific requirements including narrative statements that outline your specific "KSAs" (Knowledge, Skills, and Abilities.) Be sure to research government résumés online for specific requirements and advice before applying for a government position.

See "Avoid the Top 10 Résumé Mistakes" on page 9 also.

1. Résumés must be <u>error free</u> and well organized so that employers can easily spot what they are looking for as they scan your résumé.
   a. Approximately 75 percent of employers will remove an applicant for a typo and/or a grammatical error on a résumé.

2. Average time an employer spends reviewing your résumé is less than two minutes; some estimates are less than one minute.

3. Do use the default margin settings provided in your word processing application. For example, the default page setup for Word is 1" top and bottom margins with 1.25" right and left margins.

4. The most common font size today is 11-point font. The résumé examples that begin on page 11 use a variety of font styles and 11- or 12-point font size in the body of the résumés. It's best to never use smaller than an 11-point font in the body of your résumé.

5. Do use a variety of effects (*e.g.,* bold, underline, italics, bullets for lists), but be consistent.

6. Do use an objective <u>if</u> that objective strengthens your résumé. If 60 percent of your résumé supports your objective and if it doesn't limit your opportunities you should include one. Make sure your objective is not redundant (especially in relation to your cover letter) or overly simplistic or generic.
   a. If you do use an objective, you will need to create a specific objective for each position you apply for.

7. Do consider using a "summary statement" in your résumé, usually consisting of three bullet points that identify your valued credentials, skills, or accomplishments (see example résumé on page 12.) Remember, a <u>key goal</u> of your résumé is to differentiate yourself from the other applicants.

8. Do list education and work experience in reverse chronological order (most recent first.)

9. Do <u>not</u> use complete sentences; your résumé should be an "outline" of your qualifications and experiences, not a narrative. This means you won't need to use unnecessary words like "the" and "a" or "an."

10. Do <u>not</u> use personal pronouns such as "I" or "me" in your résumé.

11. Do include the month and year for dates of employment.

12. Do focus on the <u>transferable</u> skills you gained from work experiences:
    - Mowed lawns (a job duty)
    - Maintained outstanding relationships with customers (a transferable skill)

13. Do use parallel phrasing in describing your job duties and be concise. Begin each description of a duty using an appropriate verb and the correct verb tense. A list of these action words to describe job duties is included on page 22.

    Use present tense verbs in describing your duties for any jobs you currently hold and use past tense verbs in describing former jobs. Remember to write descriptions that describe specific skills and skill level, not simply a job duty.

14. Do <u>not</u> include hobbies or personal information. The résumé you create for employment upon completion of your college degree should not contain items related to high school.

15. Do <u>not</u> include your photo on your résumé.

16. Do keep your résumé as concise as possible. Some employers prefer one-page résumés for entry-level employees. Nearly all employers expect your résumé to be no more than two pages.
    a. If your résumé is two pages, include a header with your name at the top of the second page and the page number (see example two-page résumé, pages 14-15.)

17. For distributing your résumé in person, at a career fair, or by mail you should use high-quality bond or parchment paper in neutral colors with black ink. Do not staple if you have a two-page résumé.

    When emailing your résumé be sure to attach your résumé in the format requested (e.g. Word document, .PDF file) in the job posting. You should create a meaningful file name for your employment documents, such as *firstname_lastname_resume* and *firstname_lastname_coverletter.*

    For electronic (scannable) résumés refer to the section on scannable résumés that begins on page 18.

FORMAT

<u>Recommended sections and sequence of a chronological résumé</u>:

1. Heading – create your personal letterhead made up of your name, address, telephone number, and email address. Use your personal letterhead on all your employment documents.

2. Educational background (university name, city/state, degree, date completed or *expected* date of completion, major/minor, and GPA if appropriate.)
   a. Rule for including GPA or not – if 3.0 or higher (on 4.0 scale) then list it; or only put GPA in your major <u>if</u> above 3.0.

3. Special skills, certifications, or qualifications. You may include a list of specific computer skills, but remember most recruiters today will say you do not need to list common applications such as Word. You may choose to list related courses, training, or other areas of expertise as well.

4. Employment history, including dates (month/year), job title and duties.

5. Activities, honors/awards, or professional memberships.

6. Use a separate reference page to list your references to give to the interviewer during an interview. Your reference page is not sent with your résumé unless specifically requested. Be ready to provide your reference page at the interview.
   a. Most recruiters today will say you do not need to include "references available upon request" on your résumé.
   b. Recommended number of references to list on your reference page is 3-5 (see example reference page on page 16.)
   c. List references in alphabetical order and consistent format.

STEPS

1. Gather all necessary information including dates and names.

2. Choose the résumé format most appropriate. Reverse chronological with education listed first is the most common for college graduates.

3. Find a résumé design you like to use in creating your own résumé.

4. Prepare your résumé; proofread the résumé many times and always have at least one other person proofread it as well.

ACTIVITIES

1. Finding résumé resources:
    a. Visit your university's career services office to find information on designing effective résumés.
    b. Checkout on-line employment websites also. You can find ideas for different résumé styles and format options.
2. Create your chronological résumé to include in your employment resource portfolio (part of the Capstone Project for this unit.) Proofread your résumé several times and have at least one other person proofread it. Remember, your résumé must be *perfect!*

3. Create a two-sided business card that you can use for networking at professional and social functions (part of the Capstone Project for this unit.) Print your name, address, and vital statistics on the front of the card. Print a mini résumé on the reverse side of the card.

4. Get a consensus in your class as to whether your education or your experience is more likely to impress the recruiter or interviewer. Discuss.

RESOURCES

www.collegegrad.com – the #1 entry level job website; find entry level job opportunities along with tips on preparing your employment documents.

www.employmentwebsites.org/best-online-job-search-resources – checkout this article that identifies the best online job search resources.

www.careerbuilder.com/JobSeeker/Resources/CareerResources.aspx – Career builder's comprehensive resource center for all areas of the job hunt, preparation, and career assessment.

www.monster.com – career website where you can post your résumé and search over 1,000,000 job postings; provides 3,000 pages of résumé help, salary data, industry information, career self-assessment tests (virtual interviews, career interest inventory, job fit) and more.

www.collegerecruiter.com – college career connector service specifically for students and recent graduates where you can post your résumé and search thousands of job postings; used to find entry-level jobs and career opportunities as well as job-seeking help.

http://talentfreeway.com/ - find Michigan jobs, government jobs, internships, job fairs, and much more.

www.bestsampleresume.com – tons of sample résumés including government résumés

www.provenresumes.com/toc.html – résumé and job search tips; résumé strategies and "rate your résumé" quiz.

www.collegegrad.com/resumes – a website devoted to new college grads with sample entry level résumés, cover letters and more.

www.cover-letters.com – provides access to CareerLab's cover letter library.

www.Jobsmart.org/tools/résumé/index.htm – guide to writing résumés; includes sample résumés and links to résumé resources.

www.quintcareers.com/cover_letter_samples.html – provides sample cover letters.

http://hotjobs.yahoo.com – Yahoo's HotJobs website provides career tools and allows you to search jobs and post résumés.

www.thejobresource.com – a service for college students and recent graduates looking for entry level jobs, internships, and other opportunities.

www.jobhuntersbible.com – a supplement to the best selling book *What Color is Your Parachute*; provides access to an extensive library of resources including tests, job-hunting articles and advice, a guide to using the Internet for job searches, and links to employment information.

www.jobbankinfo.org – America's job bank provides career information and career tools, job searches, and much more.

www.bestjobsusa.com – find a job, post a résumé, employment tips, and career resources.

http://salary.com – provides salary and benefits facts and information; self-tests; links to résumé posting sites; computes and compares salaries geographically; and provides access to a wide variety of employment-related articles and resources.

Company Information Websites:

www.hoovers.com/free - provides instructions to help you find free company and industry information on the Web including financial data, recent news events, and contact information

www.glassdoor.com/index.htm - checkout company salaries, reviews, and interviews posted anonymously by employees.

www.vault.com/wps/portal/usa/companies - find out who the best companies to work for are, who offers the top internships, and what companies are the most environmentally conscious.

Relocation Websites:

www.homefair.com

www.moving.com

www.rileyguide.com/relocate.html

Avoid the Top 10 Résumé Mistakes
by Peter Vogt, Monster Senior Contributing Writer

It's deceptively easy to make mistakes on your résumé and exceptionally difficult to repair the damage once an employer gets it. So prevention is critical, especially if you've never written one before. Check out this résumé guide to the most common pitfalls and how you can avoid them.

1. Typos and Grammatical Errors
Your résumé needs to be grammatically perfect. If it isn't, employers will read between the lines and draw not-so-flattering conclusions about you, like: "This person can't write," or "This person obviously doesn't care."

2. Lack of Specifics
Employers need to understand what you've done and accomplished. For example:
   A. Worked with employees in restaurant setting
   B. Recruited, hired, trained and supervised more than 20 employees in restaurant with $2 million in annual sales

Both of these phrases could describe the same person, but the details and specifics in example B will more likely grab an employer's attention.

3. Attempting One Size Fits All
Whenever you try to develop a one-size-fits-all résumé to send to all employers, you almost always end up with something employers will toss in the recycle bin. Employers want you to write a résumé specifically for them. They expect you to clearly show how and why you fit the position in a specific organization.

4. Highlighting Duties Instead of Accomplishments
It's easy to slip into a mode where you simply start listing job duties on your résumé. For example:
- Attended group meetings and recorded minutes
- Worked with children in a day-care setting
- Updated departmental files

Employers, however, don't care so much about what you've done as what you've accomplished in your various activities. They're looking for statements more like these:
- Used laptop computer to record weekly meeting minutes and compiled them in Microsoft Word-based file for future organizational reference
- Developed three daily activities for preschool-age children and prepared them for 10-minute holiday program performance
- Reorganized 10 years' worth of unwieldy files, making them easily accessible to department members

5. Going on Too Long or Cutting Things Too Short

Despite what you may read or hear, there are no real rules governing résumé length. Why? Because human beings, who have different preferences and expectations where résumés are concerned, will be reading it.

That doesn't mean you should start sending out five-page résumés, of course. Generally speaking, you usually need to limit yourself to a maximum of two pages. But don't feel you have to use two pages if one will do. Conversely, don't cut the meat out of your résumé simply to make it conform to an arbitrary one-page standard.

6. A Bad Objective

Employers do read your résumé's objective statement, but too often they plow through vague pufferies like, "Seeking a challenging position that offers professional growth." Give employers something specific and, more importantly, something that focuses on their needs as well as your own. Example: "A challenging entry-level marketing position that allows me to contribute my skills and experience in fund-raising for nonprofits."

7. No Action Verbs

Avoid using phrases like "responsible for." Instead, use action verbs: "Resolved user questions as part of an IT help desk serving 4,000 students and staff."

8. Leaving Off Important Information

You may be tempted, for example, to eliminate mention of the jobs you've taken to earn extra money for school. Typically, however, the soft skills you've gained from these experiences (e.g., work ethic, time management) are more important to employers than you might think.

9. Visually Too Busy

If your résumé is wall-to-wall text featuring five different fonts, it will most likely give the employer a headache. So show your résumé to several other people before sending it out. Do they find it visually attractive? If what you have is hard on the eyes, revise.

10. Incorrect Contact Information

I once worked with a student whose résumé seemed incredibly strong, but he wasn't getting any bites from employers. So one day, I jokingly asked him if the phone number he'd listed on his résumé was correct. It wasn't. Once he changed it, he started getting the calls he'd been expecting. Moral of the story: Double-check even the most minute, taken-for-granted details -- sooner rather than later.

KEVIN MATTHEWS

Current Address:
1820 S. Crawford, Apt. M-320
Mount Pleasant, MI 48858
(989) 555-3000 • matthews@iserv.net

Permanent Address:
12225 Ashley
Clinton Township, MI 48038
(810) 555-1212

EDUCATION	**CENTRAL MICHIGAN UNIVERSITY,** Mount Pleasant, Michigan B.S. in Business Administration, December 20xx (expected) Major: Information Systems Minor: Applied Business Practices GPA: 3.1(4.0) overall
INTERNSHIP 5/2011 – 8/2011	**THYSSEN STEEL GROUP,** Detroit, Michigan **Intern,** *Information Technology Service Department* • Collaborated with international clients via corporate network • Provided technical information to customers • Gained troubleshooting expertise for SAP system • Worked with distribution department to expedite orders
WORK EXPERIENCE 9/2011 – present	**CENTRAL MICHIGAN UNIVERSITY,** Mount Pleasant, Michigan **Office Assistant,** *Alumni & Development Office* • Provide clerical assistance throughout academic year • Participate in annual phone-a-thon fundraisers • Assist in training all new student workers
9/2009 – 4/2011	**J. C. PENNEY,** Mount Clemens, Michigan **Sales Associate** • Developed thorough product knowledge base • Handled money and operated computerized cash register • Honored as "Associate of the Month" for August 2010
5/2008 – 8/2009	**ELIAS BROTHERS' BIG BOY,** Mount Clemens, Michigan **Wait Staff** • Operated cash register and resolved customer complaints • Assisted with new staff orientation for more than 30 staff members • Established excellent rapport with customers
KEY SKILLS	Teamwork Customer Service Leadership SAP Certification
ACTIVITIES	• American Marketing Association • Sweeney Residence Hall Council Member • Students Against Drunk Driving (President 2011 - present) • Campus Ambassador – CMU Admissions Office • Michigan Competitive Scholarship Recipient

Robert H. Beckett
(989) 400-6297
Becke1rh@cmich.edu

Campus:
200 W. Broomfield, Apt. 3-E
Mount Pleasant, MI 48858

Permanent:
625 Lincoln Avenue
Saginaw, MI 48601

OBJECTIVE: *if you choose to use an objective it must be tailored to the position*

SUMMARY
- Proficient with SPSS and Minitab statistical software
- Fluent in Spanish
- Completed specialized business courses in forensic accounting and SAP

EDUCATION Bachelor of Science in Business Administration, May 20xx (expected)
Central Michigan University, Mount Pleasant, Michigan
Double Major: Accounting and Finance
GPA: 3.43/4.00

PROJECTS Financial Analysis Research Project
- Conducted extensive research throughout semester tracking stock performance
- Analyzed stock options and comparisons
- Delivered findings and recommendations via written report and presentation

Business Communication Team Project
- Collaborated with 6-member team to develop comprehensive report and multi-media presentation on innovative business idea
- Served as team leader in delegating tasks and scheduling due dates
- Created key elements of presentation including technical aspects
- Co-produced video segment for presentation to effectively illustrate business idea

WORK EXPERIENCE

Bay Brothers – Saginaw, Michigan
Landscape Specialist
Summers 2009-present
- Assist customers with landscaping needs from recommendations to point of sale
- Answer customer telephone inquiries

ACTIVITIES: Alpha Kappa Psi Professional Business Fraternity, member, 2010-present
Leadership Safari Guide, Central Michigan University, 2010

Susan Nelson

nelson2s@cmich.edu

211 N. Main Street
Mount Pleasant, MI 48858
(989) 555-3873

459 Oak Street
Muskegon, MI 49445
(231) 555-2387

EDUCATION:

CENTRAL MICHIGAN UNIVERSITY, Mount Pleasant, Michigan
Bachelors of Science in Business Administration, May 20xx (expected)
Major: Marketing
Minor: General Business
Cumulative GPA: 3.5/4.0 (overall)

WORK EXPERIENCE:

NATIONAL CITY BANK, Mount Pleasant, Michigan
Bank Teller   8/2009 – present
- o Handle currency in all denominations
- o Provide customers with product knowledge and superior service
- o Balance drawer consistently
- o Establish strong, friendly relationships with repeat customers

LIMITED BRANDS, INC., Lansing, Michigan
Brand Sales Leader   11/2008 – 7/2009
- o Managed sales associates and oversaw interactions on sales floor
- o Reached sales goals by determining customer preferences

Brand Sales Associate   5/2008 – 11/2008
- o Initiated customer interaction through promoting brand merchandise
- o Operated computerized cash register
- o Organized inventory in stock room and on sales floor

VILLAGE FLOWERS AND GIFTS, Gladwin, Michigan
Florist   2/2006 – 5/2008
- o Designed floral arrangements
- o Developed marketing displays
- o Provided excellent service to walk-in and telephone customers

ACCOMPLISHMENTS:

- o Member – The National Society of Collegiate Scholars
- o Dean's List – 3 semesters
- o Board of Trustees Honors Scholarship, 3 semesters
- o Michigan Competitive Scholarship

- o References available upon request

RACHEL A. STREETER

6260 Summer Lane
Corunna, MI 48817

Telephone: (555) 208-2788
Email: Stree1ra@cmich.edu

OBJECTIVE: *if you choose to use an objective it must be tailored to the position*

EDUCATION

Central Michigan University, Mount Pleasant, MI
Bachelor of Science in Actuarial Science
Bachelor of Science in Business Administration
Major: Actuarial Science
Major: Accounting

Expected Graduation: May 20xx

- Dean's List, all semesters
- 3.69/4.0 GPA (overall)
- Top 10% of College Class
- Freshman and Sophomore Collegiate Scholar Athlete

Baker College, Flint, MI
General Business studies

August 2008 – July 2009

RELEVANT COURSEWORK

Calculus I, II, & III
Introduction to Analysis
Introduction to Statistics
Linear Algebra and Matrix Theory
Legal Environment of Business
Microeconomics
Macroeconomics

Applied Business Communications
Applied Statistical Methods
Insurance Planning
Financial Accounting
Managerial Accounting
Computer Programming
Global Business Communication Practices

INTERNSHIP

Auto-Owners Insurance
Lansing, MI

May 2011 – August 2011

- ➢ Developed premiums and benefits for new and enhanced insurance and annuity products
- ➢ Designed new products and product features
- ➢ Projected profitability generated by company products
- ➢ Analyzed matching of assets and liabilities including developing optimal investment strategy
- ➢ Quantified company risk exposure and proposed ways to minimize risk
- ➢ Performed actuarial research and statistical analyses

14

EMPLOYMENT

Topsy Frozen Yogurt   May 2010 - April 2011
Corunna, MI
Cashier
> ➢ Checked customers out after their yogurt experience
> ➢ Opened and closed store
> ➢ Maintained clean environment in store
> ➢ Monitored and prepared inventory daily
> ➢ Promoted newly opened business to potential customers

Embroidery Mill   Aug. 2009 - Feb. 2010
Corunna, MI
Office Assistant
> ➢ Welcomed customers and prepared orders
> ➢ Organized merchandise
> ➢ Entered store orders into computer database
> ➢ Assisted in embroidery process

CO-CURRICULAR ACTIVITIES

> ➢ Member of NCAA Division I Varsity Fastpitch Central Michigan University Softball Team, 2010 - Current
> ➢ Summer 2010 Women's Open Softball Team Manager

SKILLS

> ➢ Strong Leadership
> ➢ Organizational Skills
> ➢ Minitab
> ➢ SPSS
> ➢ Excel
> ➢ Java Programming

VOLUNTEER WORK

> ➢ YMCA Adopt-a-Family
>   -Provided meals and gifts to needy families over holidays, 2010 and 2011
> ➢ Red Cross Canned Food Drive, 2010 - 2011

References for
RACHEL A. STREETER

6260 Summer Lane
Corunna, MI 48817

Telephone: (555) 208-2788
Email: Stree1ra@cmich.edu

Ms. Janice Bannister
Internship Manager
Auto-Owners Insurance
6101 Anacapri Blvd.
Lansing, MI 48468
(517) 323-1200
Email: bannister@aowners.com

Mr. Robert Jones
Professor
Actuarial Science Program
Central Michigan University
Mount Pleasant, MI 48488
(989) 774-4000
Email: robert.jones@cmich.edu

Dr. Ellen Richards
Associate Professor
School of Accounting
Central Michigan University
Mount Pleasant, MI 48859
(989) 774-4000
Email: ellen.richards@cmich.edu

Key Points:
- Use separate reference page (typically provided at interview)
- 3-5 references listed in alphabetical order
- Provide consistent format for contact information for each reference including professional title and affiliation, email address, and phone number

Isabel Fuller

55 S. Hall Avenue ° Midland, MI 48642 ° (989) 355-2890 ° isabelfuller@gmail.com

Qualifications Summary

- ✓ Administrative professional experienced working in fast-paced and productive office environment
- ✓ Outstanding organizational and planning skills
- ✓ Extensive experience in all MS Office applications combined with comprehensive written communication skills
- ✓ Excellent interpersonal skills
- ✓ Detail oriented and resourceful

Experience Highlights

Administrative Support
- Fulfilled all administrative duties in an office setting including support functions for executive-level staff member
- Collaborated with international clients via corporate network
- Gained troubleshooting expertise for SAP system
- Developed and conducted customer satisfaction survey process providing detailed reports to upper management
- Participated in development of orientation and training for new administrative staff

Customer Service and Reception
- Worked with distribution department to expedite orders
- Provided technical information to customers and designed follow up process to increase customer satisfaction
- Greeted customers and derived pertinent information for accurate referrals and to ensure an outstanding customer service experience

Experience

CME Corporation, Mount Pleasant, MI
Executive Assistant, January 2010 - present

Days Inn and Conference Center, Mount Pleasant, MI
Administrative Assistant, May 2009 – January 2010

Ruby Tuesday, Mount Pleasant, MI
Bartender and Wait Staff, September 2008 – May 2009

Education	Community Involvement
Central Michigan University	Isabella County Soup Kitchen Volunteer
Mount Pleasant, Michigan	4-H Youth Advisor 2010 - present
B.S. in Business Administration, May 2011	Alternative Spring Break Participant Spring 2010
Major: Hospitality Services Administration	

TOPIC	**Scannable Résumé** (example page 20)
DEFINITION	A text-based or scannable résumé uses the basic form of a résumé without the formatting elements that are misread by scanners. When a job posting requests your résumé be submitted electronically, be sure to send your résumé in the format requested. Your scannable résumé is simply a no-frills version of your traditional résumé—no special formatting can be used.
RATIONALE	More and more companies are scanning résumés into their human resource databanks for quick searches, easy retrieval, and to eliminate the need to store paper copies. According to quintcareers.com, more than <u>80 percent</u> of employers are now using this scanning technology. An equal percentage of employers prefer to receive résumés by e-mail.

Scanning technology enables employers to retrieve résumés based on **key word searches** for skills and qualifications to help locate qualified candidates quickly. Some of the most common key words employers look for include *oral and written communications, teamwork* or *teambuilding, leadership, customer service, problem-solving skills,* and *decision-making skills,*

KEY POINTS

Remember—the scannable version of your résumé will not including any special formatting. The key to scannable résumés is that letters and/or characters can NOT touch each other or anything else (like a horizontal line or the "&" sign.)

1. Use a sans serif font like Arial, Courier, Futura, Helvetica, Optima, Palatino, Times, or Univers (not Times New Roman.)

2. Use the same font and font size on the entire document (11- or 12-point font recommended.)

3. Left-justify EVERY line. Maximum number of characters per line is 65.

4. Use all caps for major headings (recommended.) Use the normal arrangement of upper- and lower-case letters as appropriate within sections.

5. Avoid using special formatting such as underlines, vertical or horizontal lines. These formatting options usually result in characters that touch.

6. Do NOT use ampersands (&) or percent signs (%.)

7. Do NOT use two-column formats or lists in columnar format.

8. Use only solid bullets or hyphens; hollow bullets do not translate correctly and can be misread as characters.

9. Use specific **key words** throughout your résumé that will correspond to what employers will search for and that reflect your key skills and qualifications.

10. Use plain white paper (8 ½ x 11) only when sending out résumés that will be scanned. Send original copies only. Do <u>not</u> fold or staple (use 9 x 12 envelopes when mailing.)

11. Sending an updated résumé is acceptable, but only one time. Include a note stating that the résumé has been updated.

12. For online résumés, you should include an objective and identify the desired position.

ACTIVITIES

1. Using your chronological résumé created in the previous section, convert your chronological résumé to a scannable résumé format to include in your employment resource portfolio (part of the Capstone Project for this unit.) Your scannable résumé should contain the <u>same</u> information as your chronological résumé.

2. Design and print a two-sided business card that you can use for networking at professional and social events. On one side of the card should be your contact information, including: name, address, phone, and email. On the other side of the card should be a summarized version of your résumé.

RESOURCES

Check out the following websites that provide information about creating scannable résumés:

http://provenrésumés.com/reswkshps/electronic/scnres.html

http://www.quintcareers.com/scannable_résumés.html

http://www2.jobtrak.com/help_manuals/jobmanual/scan.html

19

KEVIN MATTHEWS
matthews@iserv.net

Current Address:
1820 S. Crawford, Apt. M-320
Mount Pleasant, MI 48858
(989) 555-3000

Permanent Address:
12225 Ashley
Clinton Township, MI 48038
(810) 555-1212

Key Points:
- Use sans serif 11- or 12-pt. font
- Each line aligns at left margin
- No use of special formatting or characters
- Make sure your email address is not underlined

EDUCATION
Central Michigan University, Mount Pleasant, Michigan
B.S. in Business Administration, December 20xx (expected)
Major: Information Systems
Minor: Marketing
GPA: 3.1(4.0) overall

INTERNSHIP
Thyssen Steel Group, Detroit, Michigan
5/2011 – 8/2011
Intern, Information Technology Service Department
-Collaborated with international clients via corporate network
-Provided technical information to customers
-Gained troubleshooting expertise for SAP system
-Worked with distribution department to expedite orders

WORK EXPERIENCE
Central Michigan University, Mount Pleasant, Michigan
9/2011 – present
Office Assistant, Alumni and Development Office
-Provide clerical assistance throughout academic year
-Participate in annual phone-a-thon fundraisers
-Assist in training new student workers

J. C. Penney, Mount Clemens, Michigan
9/2009 – 4/2011
Sales Associate
-Developed thorough product knowledge base
-Handled money and operated computerized cash register
-Honored as "Associate of the Month" for August 2010

Elias Brothers' Big Boy, Mount Clemens, Michigan
5/2008 – 8/2009
Wait Staff
-Operated cash register and resolved customer complaints
-Assisted with new staff orientation for more than 30 staff members
-Established excellent rapport with customers

KEY SKILLS
Teamwork
Customer service
Leadership
SAP Certification

ACTIVITIES
American Marketing Association
Sweeney Residence Hall Council Member
Students Against Drunk Driving, President (2011 – present)
Campus Ambassador – CMU Admissions Office
Michigan Competitive Scholarship Recipient

Action Words for Describing Job Duties

This is just a partial list of present tense verbs that can be used to create effective descriptions of job duties. Be sure to use the <u>past tense</u> form of these verbs in describing duties for jobs you no longer have.

Accomplish	Coordinate	Implement	Probe
Achieve	Convey	Improve	Process
Acquire	Correlate	Increase	Produce
Adjust	Correspond	Index	Progress
Administer	Counsel	Initiate	Promote
Advertise	Create	Institute	Purchase
Aid	Delegate	Instruct	Receive
Analyze	Design	Interview	Recommend
Approve	Detail	Insure	Reconcile
Arbitrate	Determine	Invent	Record
Arrange	Develop	Investigate	Recruit
Apply	Devise	Interview	Rectify
Assemble	Diagnose	Introduce	Reduce
Assists	Direct	Issue	Regulate
Audit	Discipline	Launch	Repair
Authenticate	Dispose	Lead	Report
Authorize	Distribute	Maintain	Research
Balance	Document	Manage	Restructure
Budget	Earn	Manufacture	Revise
Build	Edit	Market	Route
Calculate	Educate	Match	Sell
Catalog	Engineer	Merchandise	Service
Change	Enlarge	Moderate	Ship
Check	Enroll	Modify	Simplify
Close	Establish	Monitor	Solicit
Collect	Estimate	Motivate	Sort
Communicate	Evaluate	Negotiate	Standardize
Compare	Examine	Operate	Study
Complete	Expand	Order	Supervise
Compute	Facilitate	Organize	Systematize
Conceive	Forecast	Orient	Teach
Conclude	Formulate	Oversee	Test
Conduct	Generate	Plan	Train
Confirm	Govern	Post	Transfer
Consolidate	Group	Prepare	Transform
Condition	Gain	Present	Translate
Continue	Guide	Preside	Update
Contract	Handle	Price	Utilize
Control	Highlight	Program	Win
Construct	Hire	Project	Write

TOPIC **Cover Letters - Solicited and Unsolicited**
(examples pages 26-29)

DEFINITION A cover letter (sometimes called a letter of application) accompanies and introduces your résumé. A *solicited* cover letter is written when the job is advertised or the applicant *knows* of the job availability. An *unsolicited* cover letter is written when the applicant *does not know* that a job opening exists, but wishes to make the employer aware of their interest in employment for a potential *future* opening.

KEY POINTS

1. Cover letters are printed on the same quality of paper as the paper used to prepare the résumé.

2. Cover letters must be proofread carefully to be 100 percent error free. Have a friend read your cover letter and make suggestions for improvement.

3. Create your cover letter using your personal letterhead to insure you have included your contact information.

4. Keep your cover letter brief; target the job duties, skills, and requirements listed in the job posting (for solicited cover letter.) Follow the cover letter template on page 25 for format and content guidelines.

STEPS

1. Refer to the cover letter template on page 25 using block format, direct pattern.

2. In the first paragraph of a *solicited* cover letter, tell why you are writing; refer to the specific position, and tell how you heard of the opening (see pages 26 and 27 also.) If you are writing an *unsolicited* cover letter, ask a question that will get the reader's attention: "How would you like to hire an employee whose knowledge, interest, and experience in sales are top-notch? Well, I may be the one you are looking for, Ms. Lopez." (see examples page 28 and 29.

3. In the next one or two paragraphs of both a solicited and unsolicited cover letter, discuss one or two of your qualifications as they relate to the qualifications required for this position.
   a. Tell why you are particularly interested in the company, location, and/or type of work.

23

   b. Point out any related experience, specialized training, or related courses.

   c. Offer any evidence of past employment; mention anything that will give additional information concerning background and interests.

4. In the last paragraph of a *solicited* cover letter be sure to do the following:

   a. Refer the reader to your enclosed résumé.

   b. Include a request for an interview.

   c. Include specific contact information.

   d. Show appreciation.

5. In the last paragraph of an *unsolicited* cover letter be sure to do the following:

   a. Refer the reader to your enclosed résumé.

   b. If appropriate, include a call to action in your closing.

   c. Request that they keep your résumé on file for future reference.

6. Be sure to include the "enclosure" notation at the end of your letter to indicate your résumé is included.

7. Proofread your finished letter *carefully*.

   a. A good technique is to read the letter aloud and/or find someone else to read the letter aloud to you.

ACTIVITIES

1. Find a specific job posting on the Internet or newspaper to use in preparing your cover letter (part of the Capstone Project for this unit.)

   a. Prepare a *solicited* cover letter that addresses the qualifications of the job posting and follows the guidelines outlined in this section.

   b. Be sure to have at least one person proofread your cover letter.

2. Use the Internet or other resource to find samples of cover letters. Discuss your findings with other class members.

3. Write a *solicited* cover letter for an internship position in your major area of study. You will be available to intern any of the next two semesters. Attach a copy of your résumé.

4. Re-write the letter in #3 (above) as an *unsolicited* cover letter for an internship position in your major area of study.

Cover Letter Template

Personal Letterhead (your name, address, phone number(s), and email)

Date

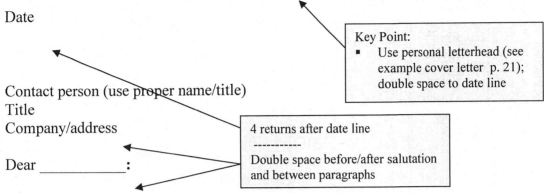

Key Point:
- Use personal letterhead (see example cover letter p. 21); double space to date line

Contact person (use proper name/title)
Title
Company/address

4 returns after date line

Double space before/after salutation and between paragraphs

Dear _____:

1ˢᵗ paragraph
- *Refer to specific position by job title and advertisement as applicable* "I am interested in .... " or "Please consider me as an applicant for ..."
- *Show knowledge of company/reputation and your desire to work there*

2ⁿᵈ-3ʳᵈ paragraph(s)
- *Relate your experiences and focus on your most significant qualifications as they relate to the job requirements*
- *Discuss your educational qualifications and skill as relevant*

last paragraph
- *Refer to your enclosed résumé; show appreciation*
- *Ask for an interview and provide contact information*

Sincerely,

Your Signature

Your name (typed)

Enclosure

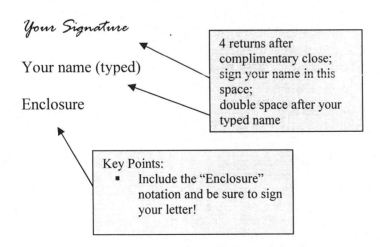

4 returns after complimentary close; sign your name in this space; double space after your typed name

Key Points:
- Include the "Enclosure" notation and be sure to sign your letter!

Roger C. Paulson
2195 Melody Drive • Mount Pleasant, MI 48858 • (989) 555-5252 • paul1rc@cmich.edu

September 1, 20xx

Ms. Daniel Alexopoulos, CPA
Enterprise Ltd.
834 Exchange Building
Lansing, MI 49873

Dear Ms. Doe:

I am interested in the Management Trainee position you have advertised on your website. I am confident I can be a great addition to the Enterprise Ltd. team. I admire your company's outstanding reputation for customer service and commitment to the environment.

To prepare for a career in management, I have completed 40 hours of business coursework at Central Michigan University. My overall grade-point average is 3.8 (on a 4-point scale.) Several management information courses I have completed also have provided me with the knowledge and skills that would be useful in working with your clients who use computers. My studies in business communication enable me to present information to clients clearly and effectively.

I believe I can be of special benefit to Enterprise Corporation because of my experience in human resources. During my internship I prepared weekly payrolls for 60 employees. My position also included the hiring of new staff members, maintaining all departmental staffing requirements, and designing a new orientation process for all new employees.

Please call me at (989) 555-5252 after you have reviewed my enclosed résumé. I would appreciate the opportunity to interview for the Management Trainee position. I look forward to speaking with you.

Sincerely,

Daniel Alexopoulos

Daniel Alexopoulos

Enclosure

RACHEL A. STREETER

6260 Summer Lane
Corunna, MI 48817

Telephone: (555) 208-2788
Email: Stree1ra@cmich.edu

March 10, 20xx

Auto-Owners Insurance
Attn: Internship Program
6101 Anacapri Blvd.
Lansing, MI 48468

Dear Sir or Madame:

Please consider me as an applicant for the Actuarial Science Internship position you have advertised on the Career Services website at Central Michigan University. My career goal is to work in the insurance industry for an industry leader like Auto-Owners. I am positive I would make a strong addition to your internship program.

In the spring of 20xx I will be graduating from Central Michigan University with a double major in Actuarial Science and Accounting. My current overall GPA is 3.69/4.0. As you can see on my enclosed résumé, the coursework I have completed has prepared me for an actuarial science internship. I have a strong aptitude for working with numbers, research, analysis, and critical thinking. I have earned a 4.0 in my statistics courses and am proficient with statistical analysis software, both Minitab and SPSS.

My extensive studies in both the actuarial science and accounting fields, has given me the knowledge and skills necessary for success as an actuarial science intern. I have learned to be extremely focused on my studies and maintain a high GPA while also being a Division I varsity athlete on CMU's Women's Softball Team. Having many demands on my time has taught me to be organized and to manage my time efficiently. I have also developed strong team skills and effective written and oral communication skills.

Please contact me at (555) 208-2788 after you have reviewed my résumé and application. I would appreciate the opportunity to interview for an Actuarial Science Internship position at Auto-Owners Insurance. I look forward to hearing from you.

Sincerely,

Rachel A. Streeter

Rachel A. Streeter

Enclosure

Jessica L. Morales
Moral1jl@cmich.edu

1301 Washington St., Mount Pleasant, MI 48858   **Phone: (989) 775-5555**

September 9, 20xx

Salomon Smith Barney
500 Northland Drive
Lansing, Michigan 48075

Dear Sir or Madame:

I am interested in a position in the financial services field at your firm. I have researched Salomon Smith Barney and I am impressed with your benefits package and the freedom to earn unlimited income. I feel my studies at Central Michigan University have prepared me for a career in financial services.

I am confident of my ability to learn rapidly and retain information. Critical thinking, problem-solving and many clerical skills add to my experience. I am detail-oriented and a team player. I feel I would be an asset to Salomon Smith Barney.

I have enclosed a copy of my résumé for your review. Please keep my résumé on file for future reference. Feel free to contact me when a position is available. Thank you for your time.

Sincerely,

Jessica L. Morales

Jessica L. Morales

Enclosure

> Key Points:
> - 1st paragraph - state your interest in an <u>area</u> or <u>department</u> (e.g. financial services field, marketing department, etc.) rather than a specific position
>
> - Last paragraph - ask them to keep your résumé on file for when a position becomes available

Roger C. Paulson

2195 Melody Drive • Mount Pleasant, MI 48858 • (989) 555-5252 • paul1rc@cmich.edu

October 1, 20xx

Ms. Constance Wayland
Human Resources Director
Direct Resource Marketing, Inc.
9874 West Patriot Street
Punxsutawney, PA 39874

Dear Ms. Wayland:

Are you looking for a person who can make effective sales calls and provide imaginative merchandising displays? My marketing degree and practical experience in sales and merchandising has prepared me for a successful career with Direct Resource Marketing.

Practical work as a marketing field representative during my internship gave me the opportunity to plan and execute effective sales promotions to increase product sales. I successfully opened new accounts and secured the best floor displays. I have also conducted route analyses and set up key account systems.

An integral part of my marketing experience has involved frequent contact with retailers. I have an excellent record of success in dealing with clients to achieve assigned sales goals.

I would appreciate an opportunity to discuss my qualifications with you at your convenience. I have enclosed my résumé for your review. I can be reached at (989) 555-4450. Please keep my résumé on file for future reference.

Sincerely yours,

Roger C. Paulson

Roger C. Paulson

Enclosure

Thank-You Letter (example page 32)

A brief thank-you letter should always be sent after an interview to show appreciation, good manners, and perseverance.

       a. Most importantly, a thank-you letter will help you to stand out from other candidates (only about 5 percent of candidates actually send a thank-you letter.)

       b. A traditional letter is still the most common form of a thank-you letter, but email is considered acceptable. Base your decision on the company culture.

       c. Be sure you ask the interviewer for his/her business card to be certain you have the necessary information.

KEY POINTS

1. Send a thank-you letter (or email) promptly after an interview (within 24 hours ideally.) If mailing a thank-you letter, it may be typed or handwritten. Use your judgment in determining the formality you feel is most appropriate.

2. Refer to the interviewer's business card for correct title, address, and proper spelling of name.

3. If interviewed by more than one person, send a thank-you letter/email to each interviewer. You can send essentially the same letter to each interviewer, but change 1-2 sentences to individualize each letter.

4. Use the direct pattern in your thank-you letter or email. The first sentence should thank the interviewer for his/her time; refer to the interview date and the specific position for which you interviewed.

5. You should mention a topic discussed during the interview or refer to the positive impression made by some aspect of the interview.

6. Mention a skill or strength you have for the position that you did not have the chance to discuss during the interview.

7. Refer to any recent award or accomplishment that relates to the job requirements that you may have forgotten to mention during the interview.

8. Conclude the letter by restating your interest in the job; if you are no longer interested in the job, now is the time to share this information as well.

STEPS

1. Use proper format outlined on page 25.

2. Use direct pattern and be brief.

3. End with a positive, forward-looking statement.

4. Proofread your letter carefully and be sure to sign it.

ACTIVITIES

1. Interview an employer or human resource professional and ask him/her the following questions:
   a. Do you think it's important that interviewees send thank-you letters? Why?
   b. What percentage of applicants interviewed by you or your company would you estimate sends thank-you letters?
   c. Discuss the key points from your interview in class.

2. Create a thank-you letter for an interview based on the job posting you used for your cover letter to include in your employment resource portfolio (part of the Capstone Project for this unit.)
   a. Proofread your letter carefully; ask a classmate to proof the letter also.

Patrick Jones
Jonesp07@hotmail.com

1280 Maple Street
Mount Pleasant, MI 48858

April 30, 20xx

Date line is first typed line after letterhead; then 4 returns to name and address of recipient

Mr. Kevin McLaughlin
Simkins Financial Group
800 Glenview Parkway
Clare, MI 48617

Dear Ms. Stevens:

Thank you for the opportunity to interview with you for the accounting position on Monday, April 29.

I enjoyed learning more about Simkins Financial Group and the accounting department. I was impressed by the friendly atmosphere and enjoyed meeting the accounting staff. The accounting courses I have recently completed were especially relevant to the challenges of a financial services organization.

Now that I have a better understanding of the responsibilities of your accounting department, I am confident that my qualifications and skills would be a real contribution to the team at Simkins Financial Group. My education and work experience in the accounting field have given me the real world experience you seek. I look forward to hearing from you soon.

Sincerely,

Patrick Jones

Patrick Jones

TOPIC **Cleaning up Your Digital Dirt**

EXPLANATION Digital dirt is a term used to describe unflattering personal information that may be found on the Internet. The vast majority of recruiters are using search engines to check on candidates. In many cases where digital dirt has been unearthed by employers, the candidate was not offered the job.

ACTIVITIES

1. Type your name into different search engines to find out what employers would find out about you with a few simple keystrokes. Search on your name using Google.com, Yahoo.com, MSN.com, and Pipl.com to see what employers might find out about you.

2. Clean up any negative information about you on the Internet whenever possible. In some cases you can contact the website's owner and ask to have these things removed.

3. Clean up all information you have on any social-networking websites like Facebook and MySpace, especially photographs. Employers have devised ways to access these sites and search for information on job candidates.

4. Read more about how your digital dirt can affect your chances for finding a job and how to clean up your digital dirt at www.cfo.com/article.cfm/5404994 and www.msnbc.msn.com/id/26904049/ns/business-careers.

TOPIC   **Evaluating Job Offers**

EXPLANATION   Listed below are factors you will want to consider when determining whether or not you will accept a position. While salary is an important factor, be sure you weigh your starting salary against the salary potential of the position and against the cost of living of the geographic area where you plan to live. Also, consider these factors:

Job/Employer Related Factors
- Potential for career advancement
- Work schedule (traditional "9:00 - 5:00" or flexible hours)
- Work environment/attire (formal vs. informal)
- Bonus or commission plans
- Benefits such as profit sharing, 401K plan, and insurance
- Travel
- Reputation and stability of employer
- Size of employer
- Ability to gain a mentor
- Type of industry

Geographic/Life-Style Factors
- Geographic location
- Climate
- Social life for singles, couples or family
- Commute to work
- Availability of suitable housing
- Size and type of community (suburban, metropolitan, rural)

Source: http://www.careerfairs.com/tips/evaloffers.asp

ACTIVITIES

1. Read more about evaluating a job offer and take a quiz to determine what's most important to you when considering an offer at http://jobsearch.about.com/od/salaryinformation/a/joboffer.htm.

TOPIC   **Letter Accepting a Position** (example page 36)

DEFINITION   A letter accepting a position with a company should be written when you accept the job.

EXPLANATION   A letter accepting a position is considered a "good news" letter.
    a. Use the *direct* style of writing.
    b. Be brief.

STEPS

1. Use personal letterhead with the proper date line, address of the recipient, and salutation.

2. Place the acceptance in the first sentence of your first paragraph.

3. Keep the letter short and simple.

4. Close with a positive, forward-looking statement.

5. Be sure to include the "enclosures" notation if including other documents with your letter.

6. Proofread very carefully.
    a. Read the letter aloud; then read the letter to another person.

ACTIVITIES

1. Look at the jobs available advertisements in the recent edition of a local newspaper. Find a job that you think you would like. Assume that you have been offered the job by the company. Write the job acceptance letter.

2. Search the Internet to find a sample of a job acceptance letter. How is the letter the same or different from the one you wrote? Write a memo to your instructor telling he or she what you have found (refer to memo format guidelines in Unit III.)

3. Assume that you have been successful in getting an internship for the next semester. Write a letter accepting the internship to the company who offered that internship to you.

KEVIN MATTHEWS

Current Address:
1820 S. Crawford, Apt. M-320
Mount Pleasant, MI 48858
(989) 555-3000

Permanent Address:
12225 Ashley
Clinton Township, MI 48038
(810) 555-1212

June 1, 20xx

Mr. Juan A. Jobb, Manager
Human Resources Division
Jobb Products, Inc.
76 North Bailey Road
Tyler, TX 78900

Dear Mr. Jobb:

I accept, with pleasure, your offer of a job in the Information Systems Division of Jobb Products.

Enclosed is the information you requested from me along with the reference letters from three former employers.

Working for your company has always been a goal of mine; thank you so much for the offer. I look forward to many long years of employment with Jobb Products.

Sincerely,

Kevin Matthews

Kevin Matthews

Enclosures

TOPIC	**Letter Rejecting a Position** (example page 38)

DEFINITION When you receive a job offer that you cannot accept, you should write an indirect (inductive) style letter turning down the job. Be as pleasant as you can because you may one day be looking for another job, and you may want to consider another offer—perhaps one you rejected in the past.

EXPLANATION A letter of rejection is prepared using an indirect style. Use personal letterhead with the proper date line, address of the recipient, and salutation. Your signature appears at the bottom beneath the complimentary close.

KEY POINTS

1. Use block format; direct pattern.

2. Use a buffer; start with a neutral opening that does not give a hint that the bad news is coming.

3. Provide reasons, explanation, or facts. Give the reason(s) why you cannot accept the job.

4. Tell the reader that, for the reasons just listed, you are sorry that you cannot accept the job.

5. Close in a pleasant way and include your thanks.

6. Proofread very carefully.

ACTIVITIES

1. Prepare a letter refusing a job offered to you.

2. Search the Internet for additional information about proper etiquette for refusing a job offer.

3. You were successful in your interviewing for an internship next semester; in fact, you were offered *two* internships. Write a letter *accepting* the one internship and a letter *rejecting* the other offer.

37

Kellie Corelli

1950 North Shore Drive • Port Hope, MI 48468 • (517) 555-5252 • kellieseritt@hotmail.com

May 31, 20xx

Ms. Isadora Montez
Director of Marketing Research
The Montez Corporation
98765 South Boulder Street
Grand Forks, ND 54701

Dear Ms. Montez:

The interview I had with you last week was exciting and interesting. Your company is certainly on the cutting edge of the latest happenings in marketing research.

Your offering me the job was much appreciated; but, as I pointed out to you and the others who interviewed me, I am looking for a position that has a major emphasis in international sales. As a result, I am taking a job with Sellers Unlimited, where I will be the international director of sales.

Thank you so much for the interview and the job offer.

Sincerely,

Kellie Corelli

Kellie Corelli

TOPIC   **Application Follow-up Letter** (example page 40)

DEFINITION   An application follow-up letter is one sent to a company when you have not heard from that company and you want to know what happened to your application.

BACKGROUND   The application follow-up letter is written in direct style. You have not heard from the company, so you write a letter.

    a. Usually wait four to six weeks before you write the letter to give the company ample time to reply.

    b. Make the letter short and to the point. Tell the reader something new that you have done since you last wrote to the company.

KEY POINTS

1. Use block format; direct pattern.

2. Keep your letter brief.

3. Tell the reader something else you have done since you last talked to him or her.

4. Remind the reader that you want your application kept on file.

5. Proofread and edit the letter carefully.

ACTIVITIES

1. Write a letter to follow up an interview you had with a company several weeks ago. You have not heard from the company, and you want them to keep your application on file.
Supply a name and address.

2. Check the Internet to see if you can find samples of application follow-up letters. How can you incorporate some of the information you found into your application follow-up letter?

3. Write a letter to follow up on an application you sent in several weeks ago. You have heard nothing from the company.

Nancy Kawalski
nekawak27@yahoo.com

7654 North Main Avenue
Grand Rapids, MI 49503

August 1, 20xx

Mr. Roger McIntyre
Director of Personnel
McIntyre Products, Inc.
987 Oak Boulevard
Fargo, ND 58132

Dear Mr. McIntyre:

Since our last discussion about a month ago, I have completed a marketing research course at the local community college. In addition, I am now enrolled in the advanced marketing research class at Central Michigan University.

Please keep my application active in your files. I am still interested in the position you have available, and I look forward to hearing from you soon.

Enclosed is an updated copy of my résumé for your files.

Sincerely,

Nancy Kawalski

Nancy Kawalski

Enclosure

Letter of Recommendation (example page 43)

You may be asked to write a letter of recommendation by one of your friends or employees, or you may ask someone to write a letter of recommendation for you.

EXPLANATION A letter of recommendation is usually written in the *direct* style because the letter should be a positive one. If you are asked to give a recommendation for someone and you only have unfavorable news, then do not give the recommendation.

KEY POINTS

Opening Paragraph

   a. Name the applicant and the position sought.

   b. Tell the reader that your remarks are confidential.

   c. Describe your relationship with the candidate (fellow worker, former colleague, former subordinate, etc.)

Body of the Letter

   1. Describe the applicant's performance.

   2. State what you think the applicant's potential is.

   3. Include statements about organizational skills, people skills (does the applicant work well with people?) and communication skills.

   4. Mention some of the tasks or projects the applicant has completed.

Closing

   1. Summarize the candidate's strengths.

   2. Rank the candidate. (Of all the marketing research people I have recommended, Maria ranks in the top 10 percent.)

   3. Offer to supply additional information, if necessary. Provide a phone number or email address where you can be contacted for more information, if needed.

1. Sometimes when you ask someone to write a letter of recommendation, he or she may say something like "Go ahead and write the letter for me; then I'll read and sign it." So, write a letter recommending yourself to an employer who is looking for someone with your skills and abilities.

2. Check out the Internet for examples of letters of recommendation and suggestions for writing a letter of recommendation. Prepare a short memo on suggestions for writing the recommendation letter, and read the memo to your classmates for comments and suggestions.

3. Write a recommendation letter for a co-worker and good friend of yours for a position with another company. The position is a step up from the one the person currently holds. Supply a name and address of the recipient. Assume any facts you need to complete the recommendation letter.

4. Your college roommate has asked you to write a letter of recommendation for an internship that is available during the summer. Assume any facts and information you wish, and write a letter of recommendation for your roommate. Supply a name and address of the recipient.

Dr. Robert T. Allison, Associate Professor
Central Michigan University, Mount Pleasant, MI 48859

allis2rt@cmich.edu
(989) 774-4000

May 29, 20xx

Ms. Rosa Portales, Sales Director
Portales Enterprises, Inc.
12345 Main Avenue
Mount Pleasant, MI 48858

Dear Ms. Portales:

At the request of Sandra Simon, I submit to you a confidential letter of recommendation to support her application for the position of Assistant Sales Director at Portales. Ms. Simon was a student in my business communication class at Central Michigan University during the 2006-2007 academic year.

Sandra's outstanding performance in my classroom is a strong indication of her work ethic on the job. Many students who have excelled in my class have succeeded well beyond my expectations in their current career. Not only was Sandra well organized and well prepared for every class, but she also communicated her thoughts and opinions in an efficient and effective manner. Every project and task that was handed out was completed on time and done with great detail to directions.

Sandra is a diligent worker as well as an intelligent and respectful person. Of all the students I have taught over the years, Sandra ranks among the top 5 percent. If you need additional information, please call me at (989) 774-4000.

Sincerely,

Robert T. Allison

Robert T. Allison
Associate Professor of Marketing
Central Michigan University

| **TOPIC** | **Interviewing** |

EXPLANATION

Interviews are typically conducted in two ways—structured or unstructured. <u>Preparation</u> is the key to your success in any interview. Planning for the common interview questions and the type of interview questions (e.g. behavioral) you may be asked is most important.

1. Structured interviews consist of the same questions asked in the same sequence of each interviewee.

2. Unstructured interviews are informal and questions can vary from one applicant to another.

3. Trained recruiters structure interviews in three sections:
   a. Establishing cordial relationship
   b. Eliciting information from you
   c. Providing information about the job and company

4. Remember, the interviewer will try to determine the answer to three basic questions during the interview:
   a. Can you do the job?
      -Do you possess the necessary skills to succeed in this job and at this company?
      -Interviewers will most likely use behavioral interview questions to determine if you have the necessary skills.
   b. Will you do it?
      -How do your soft skills measure up?
      -Impress your interviewer with enthusiasm, passion, and motivation.
   d. Will you fit in?
      -Do you have what it takes to work well with others?

KEY POINTS

1. Preparation for an interview is the key to a successful interview. The more prepared you are, the more poised and confident you will be during the interview. To succeed in the interview you will need to:
   a. Conduct company research.
   b. Prepare your answers to common interview questions.
   c. Practice your answers and your introduction.
   d. Prepare your own questions to ask the interviewer.
   e. Plan and prepare for what you will wear to the interview.
   f. Take copies of your résumé to the interview in a portfolio.
   g. Arrive 15 minutes before the interview is scheduled to begin.

        h. Be sure to stand up when you meet your interviewer.
        i. Let the interviewer lead the interview at all times.

2. Research the company. The first thing you should do is thoroughly research the company's website. In addition, you will need to research "unbiased" sources of information about the company. Utilize the many resources available online to search for information and news about the company from a variety of reputable sources.

   Typical topics you would want to research would include the company history, who owns them/who they own, locations including their headquarters, and the size of the company (including the number of employees, number of locations/offices/stores.) You should also research employment-related issues such as advancement opportunities, employee benefits, and the company's reputation as an employer and in the community.

   Check websites like www.hoovers.com/free/ and http://finance.yahoo.com/ for financial information on the company, their financial history, and current information such as stock value, earnings, recent trends, growth or down sizing.

3. Prepare your answers to common interview questions. The best way to do this is to first outline your answers to the common interview questions provided at the end of this unit; then practice your answers.

4. Prepare for different types of interview questions. Traditional interview questions are straight-forward questions. Behavioral interview questions are designed to determine if you possess the skills and behaviors the employer is looking for. Behavioral interviews are designed to identify past behaviors as a predictor of future behaviors. Example behavioral interview questions are also included at the end of this unit.

   Use a system like the "BAR" method when responding to behavioral interview questions. This will ensure you respond thoroughly to each question. In using the BAR method your response will consist of three parts: "B" – background; "A" – action; "R" – results.

   Focus on success stories and/or experiences that illustrate your skills and the skills an employer would be looking for (particularly those listed for the job you will be interviewing for.) Provide thorough, complete answers to behavior questions that answer the three components of the BAR method.

- Put together a list of your KSAs (Knowledge, Skills, and Abilities) and positive traits – focus on things that will set you apart from others.
- Target the skills employers value most by reviewing the list of these skills on page 52.
- Avoid the common interview mistakes by reviewing the list on page 53.

5. Prepare for the interview by practicing your answers to common interview questions with a friend.

6. Prepare your own questions to ask the interviewer regarding the position, the company, and when the hiring decision is made. You'll need to research the company thoroughly to be prepared with quality questions.

7. Plan and prepare for what you will wear to the interview. Make sure everything you wear is clean and pressed. Polish your shoes and be comfortable in what you wear. Dress professionally and appropriately for the type of position and/or the industry. For example, you would expect banking professionals to be dressed more conservatively than those in retail. When in doubt, be conservative with your wardrobe choices. The interviewer will form an opinion of you based on your appearance within the first few seconds of the interview.

8. Take only a portfolio to the interview with copies of your résumé and reference list to give the interviewer(s).

9. Arrive 15 minutes early. Be on your best behavior before, during, and after the interview (you may be observed in the parking lot and/or the reception area.) Practice your introduction and handshake in advance.

Remember that the interviewer is likely to form their opinion of you in the first few seconds they meet you. Research indicates that approximately 93 percent of a person's communication effectiveness is determined via nonverbal communication.

10. Be sure to stand up when you meet your interviewer. Use a firm but painless handshake with two to three "pumps". Use direct eye contact and smile—it indicates confidence. Introduce yourself with a greeting such as "good morning".

11. Let the interviewer lead the interview at all times. Expect to do about 50 percent of the talking during the interview. Use the interviewer's name, smile and lean forward when listening

or talking during the interview. Use a strong, confident voice. Be enthusiastic! Pause as needed to organize your thoughts before answering open ended questions. Ask good questions about the job and/or the company that you prepared in advance.

Find out the date for their final decision and/or how and when to follow up before the interview concludes. Get the interviewer's business card or contact information. Thank the interviewer and shake his/her hand again when leaving.

Send a thank-you letter or to your interviewer(s) as soon as possible (24 hours is ideal.) Email is also an appropriate way to send your thank-you letter.

ACTIVITIES

1. Prepare your answers to one of the lists of common interview questions provided at the end of this unit (part of the Capstone Project for this unit.) Outline your answers to each question, avoiding complete sentences. Take an inventory of your skills, experiences, and knowledge. Focus on providing specific examples that demonstrate how you have applied or developed these attributes.

2. Complete a practice interview on Quintessential Careers website at http://www.quintcareers.com/interview_question_database/. Choose the type of interview question you want to practice then enter your response to each question in the spaces provided. Submit your responses by pressing the submit button. Print out a copy of the response page so you'll have a copy of your answers. You'll be sent a sample excellent response for each question. Compare how you answered each interview question with the sample responses. Turn in a copy of your answers and the sample responses to your instructor.

3. Conduct Internet research on websites like Monster.com and Careerbuilder.com to compile a list of common interview mistakes. Discuss this topic in class.

4. Conduct Internet research to learn more about behavioral interview questions and the best strategies for answering these questions. Read more about behavioral interviews and behavioral interviewing strategies at www.quintcareers.com/sample_behavioral.html.

5. Conduct research to find out how to prepare for a career fair. Prepare your "30-second commercial" for a career fair interview. Include the following things in your "commercial"-- introduce yourself, your major, your university, when you will

graduate, and discuss the skills and knowledge you possess that are most desired by employers.

6. Conduct research on a specific company according to the directions given by your instructor. Follow the assignment on conducting company research on pages 49-50.

Company Research Assignment

What should you look for when researching a potential employer?

You'll be interviewing for a position with _____ next week. Conduct some company research on this company so you will be prepared for your interview. Use the resources outlined below, in addition to this company's website, to find information about each topic.

Turn in your answers to each of the questions as instructed (be sure to type the question and your answer.) Study your research and be sure you are familiar with the company before your interview.

Topics to Research

Typical topics you would want to research about a potential employer would include the company history, type of business, who owns them, where headquarters are located, the size of the company (including the number of employees and locations); what are the potential career paths/career growth; are there any employment issues such as the company's reputation as an employer, employee benefits, or any bad publicity; and financial information such as stock value, earnings, recent trends, and growth or down sizing.

Tips and some suggested resources for conducting effective company research:

- Every public company has "investor" information on their website, which is always a good place to start and to learn about the financial information of the company.

- Some websites require a membership fee and registration (*e.g.* Hoovers and Morningstar) but these websites also provide a great deal of information at no charge (see below.)

- Yahoo! Finance (free) – provides stock quotes, stock symbol lookup, company profiles, business summary, competition, articles, and more. http://finance.yahoo.com/

- Morningstar website ($$) – provides investor-types of information including the ability to search their database for recent articles on companies. http://morningstar.com/ *register yourself for "free member" privileges.

- Hoover's website ($$) – provides research for over 13 million companies and 600 industries. Many areas of this website (*e.g.* click on "research companies and industries" tab) will provide lots of useful free information. This link below will provide free information on 124 public companies: http://www.hoovers.com/global/co/today.xhtml?type=public&page=1

Company Research Assignment - continued

Topics to Research:
1. Is the company public or private?

2. What does the company do?
   -Yahoo! Finance
   -if the company sells products, see Hoovers' website to find the basic information
    about almost every product sold in U.S.

3. Who runs the company?

4. What is the current stock price?

5. How has their stock done in the last 5 years?
      -Morningstar.com

6. Who does the company compete against?
      -Yahoo! Finance; http://finance.yahoo.com/

7. How many employees do they have?

8. Search for any news articles about this company from reputable sources. What are the
   topics of the five most recent articles and the date of each article? Find at least one
   article that discusses a problem or something negative about the company.

9. What is their mission statement?

10. What are the entry-level employment opportunities?

http://jobsearch.about.com/cs/interviews/a/behavioral.htm – your resource for behavioral interviews, the questions and answers; explains the behavioral interview process and what the employer is looking for in your answers to these questions.

www.quintcareers.com/interview_question_database/ - Quintessential Careers website is an outstanding resource for all aspects of your job search. This link will take you to their database of 150 interview questions (traditional and behavioral.) You can also go through sample interview questions with samples of excellent responses, and review situational interview questions.

www.job-interview.net - provides a complete interview guide plus interview questions and answers.

http://content.monster.com/Interview/Home.aspx - provides lots of information for all aspects of the interview, including fashion mistakes, how hobbies can help you, response strategies, keeping your cool, curve-ball questions, what questions to ask, the ten interview errors, questions they should not ask, phone interviews, and interviewers' pet peeves.

What skills or abilities do employers value most in employees?

The American Management Association (AMA) surveyed employers to determine what skills are most highly desired by employers for the 21st Century workforce. According to the *AMA 2010 Critical Skills Survey,* executives identified these four critical skills (the "four Cs") as crucial to workforce preparedness and business success:

1. Communication skills

2. Critical thinking

3. Creativity

4. Collaboration

A survey of hundreds of recruiting professionals conducted each year by the National Association of Colleges and Employers (NACE) determines what types of major companies will be hiring for entry-level positions and what skills or abilities they're looking for in candidates. According to the NACE survey, recruiters identified the following 11 skills as the most desirable skills and abilities for entry-level positions:

1. Oral communication skills

2. Interpersonal skills

3. Analytical skills

4. Teamwork skills

5. Flexibility

6. Computer skills

7. Proficiency in field of study

8. Written communication skills

9. Leadership skills

10. Work experience

11. Internship or cooperative education experience

Six Interview Mistakes
Written by Monster Contributing Writer Michael Neece

Avoid the typical interview traps by understanding the purpose and expectations of an interview. Here are six common interview traps to watch out for.

1. **Confusing an interview with an interrogation.**

   An interview is not an interrogation. Don't confuse the two! In an interrogation, only one person asks the questions and the other gives the answers. An interview is a business conversation where both people ask and answer questions. If you expect to be interrogated and don't ask any questions, you'll leave the interviewer in the reluctant role of interrogator.

2. **Making a so-called weakness seem positive.**

   One of the most common interview questions is "what are your weaknesses?" Conventional interview wisdom advises you to highlight a weakness like "I'm a perfectionist," and turn it into a positive. Interviewers aren't always impressed because they've heard this answer many times. The better approach to this question is to highlight a skill you wish to improve upon and describe what you are doing to enhance this skill. Interviewers don't care what your weaknesses are, they want to see how you handle the question and what your answer indicates about you.

3. **Failing to ask questions.**

   Every interview concludes with the interviewer asking if you have any questions. The worst thing to say is that you don't have any! This indicates you are not interested and are not prepared. Interviewers are more impressed by the questions you ask than the selling points you try to make. Make a list of questions <u>you</u> want to ask at the interview ahead of time.

4. **Researching the company but not yourself.**

   Candidates intellectually prepare by researching the company. Most candidates don't do the same preparation in researching themselves and taking inventory of their skills, experience, and knowledge. Formulate a talent inventory and write down an example from your life that demonstrates each. Remember to include technical skills, software applications, and discipline specific tools.

5. **Leaving your cell phone on.**

   A ringing cell phone is not appropriate for an interview. Turn it off (don't leave it on and set it to vibrate) before you enter the building. Better yet, don't even take it with you.

6. **Waiting for a call.**

   Time is your enemy after the interview. After you send a thank-you email and note to every interviewer, follow up a couple days later with either a question or additional information. Contact the person who can hire you and not the HR department. HR is famous for not returning calls. You goal is to keep everyone's memory of you fresh.

| **TOPIC** | **Meal Interview and Dining Etiquette** |

EXPLANATION

Interviews over lunch or dinner are gaining in popularity. If part of your interview involves dining out, be sure to review proper dining etiquette beforehand (resources are given on page 55 also.) During a meal interview you need to focus on answering questions confidently and intelligently while also paying attention to how you look while eating. Proper table manners are essential. Brush up on your etiquette before the interview as needed. Always be polite and maintain formality throughout the meal.

KEY POINTS

1. No personal items should be on the table when dining; no keys, no purses, no folders. Don't even bring your cell phone into the restaurant!
2. Be aware – no elbows on the table, don't chew with your mouth open or talk with food in your mouth.
3. Be polite – say please and thank you to everyone, including the wait staff.
4. Brush up on table manners before the interview to be prepared and confident.
5. Order carefully – follow the lead from your interviewer and order something in the same price range and the same number of courses. Avoid messy or difficult foods to eat. Order foods that are easy to eat with a knife and fork.
6. Talk and eat – wait for everyone at the table to be served before you begin eating. Not eating can indicate nervousness. Don't just answer questions. Ask questions to give yourself the chance to eat.
7. Ending the meal – it is never appropriate to ask for a doggy bag in this situation. Don't offer to pay. Reaffirm your interest to the interviewer combined with a handshake and "thank you." Follow up with a thank-you letter or email the next day.

ACTIVITIES

1. Do you know about proper job-hunting etiquette? Take the online etiquette quiz at http://quintcareers.com/job-hunting_etiquette_quiz.html to test your knowledge on a variety of business etiquette areas. Test your etiquette further, including dining etiquette with the quiz at www.rasolutions.net/quick-dining-quiz.htm.

RESOURCES

The Etiquette Advocate – founded in 2004 to assist corporations, organizations, schools, and individuals in mastering social etiquette, business and international protocol, and dining etiquette skills: www.etiquetteadvocate.com/

Take a copy of this dining etiquette tip sheet with you: www.k-state.edu/ces/students/documents/workshopdining etiquettebrochure.pdf

Table manners: http://cms.bsu.edu/About/AdministrativeOffices/CareerCenter/MyCar eerPlan/ProfDev/ProfImageEtiquette/DiningEtiquette.aspx

International business culture and etiquette: www.executiveplanet.com/

TOPIC   **Telephone Interview**

EXPLANATION   Many companies use telephone interviews as a screening technique to save time and money. This type of interview is typically brief (20-30 minutes) with one or more interviewers. Telephone interviews can be challenging because you have no visual connection to your interviewer(s). Without nonverbal cues and body language to observe it is difficult to gauge your performance. If you are invited for a face-to-face interview, you know you succeeded.

Prepare for a telephone interview the same way as you would any other interview, but with a few additions and modifications explained below.

KEY POINTS

1. Treat the phone interview as seriously you would for an in-person interview. Don't be casual or informal. Research the company and prepare your responses. Stand up or sit up straight at a table or desk to improve your psychological frame of mind. Dress up and you will feel more confident and professional.

2. Have your résumé, cover letter, and the job posting in front of you. Bring any other notes that will help you remember any key points, skills, or experiences you want to be sure to mention.

3. Use a high-quality phone. Cell phones do not always have the best quality reception or dependability.

4. Arrange for complete privacy and ensure there will be no interruptions during the interview.

ACTIVITIES

1. Read about the "six interview mistakes" on page 53. Prepare five questions you would ask at a job interview to avoid making mistake #3 on the list. Next, prepare your "talent inventory" outlining your experience, skills, and knowledge to avoid making mistake #4.

2. Go to www.job-interview.net. Click on "mock job interviews" and follow the instructions to complete a mock interview based on specific career fields, actual job openings, and job description. Each mock interview includes a practice question set, answer tips, and interview resources. This website also provides great interview tips, answers to 900+ possible interview questions, and questions to ask the interviewer.

3. Searching for information about a company is in some ways a treasure hunt. After you have narrowed your job search down to one or two companies, you may wish to do a thorough investigation of the company. Find a company to work for that is a good fit for you. Good research will help you find the right fit and provide you with excellent information about the company.

   At the end of this activity is a list of company directories, both national and international that will aid you in your job search. Here are some of the items you will want to investigate. Perhaps you will find other items not listed here that will be helpful to you in your investigation.

   a. Name of the company.
   b. Short history and background of the company.
   c. Location of home office, president's name, and number or employees.
   d. Branch offices.
   e. Ranking of company from the *Fortune* list.
   f. The current price and the high and low range of the company stock for this year (assuming the company is listed on a stock exchange.)
   g. The current P/E ratio.
   h. A company brochure or a company fact sheet. What is included in the brochure or fact sheet?
   i. What is the latest business plan?

4. Write a job description for which you could apply. Items to be included in a job description may include the following:
   a. Job title
   b. Job responsibilities and duties
   c. Degree required
   d. Skills involved
   e. Working environment
   f. Salary

5. This assignment incorporates the use of the Internet, a trip or two to the library, and perhaps even a call or letter to the company itself. Some students in the past have been invited in to talk to one of the officers. Companies like the idea of helping students complete a project because the company image is being promoted at the same time.

   Prepare the report under the direction of your instructor, who will suggest a proper format for presenting your data.

Company Directories

Directory of Corporate Affiliations. (Annual.) Providence, NJ: National Register Publishing.

Million Dollar Directory: America's Leading Public & Private Companies (Annual.) Parsippany, NJ: Dun and Bradstreet.

Moody's Manuals. (Annual, with semiweekly supplements.) New York: Moody's Investors Service.

Standard and Poor's Register of Corporations, Directors and Executives. (Annual.) New York: Standard and Poor's.

Ward's Business Directory of U.S. Private and Public Companies. (Annual.) Detroit: Gale Research.

World Business Directory. Detroit: Gale Research.

6. Study four of the company directories listed in #5 above. Compare each of the four as to what type of information they contain and how these sources can be helpful to you in your job search. Submit a memo of your comparisons to your instructor.

7. How well do you know yourself? How well do you understand yourself? Self-evaluation can help you determine what you are looking for in a job. Below are several questions that should provide you with a look at what you are really after in terms of a job. Recruiters may ask you some of these questions, but the purpose of this exercise is to get to know what you really want in a job.

   Write out answers to the following questions. Then in a few months, write out the answers to the following questions again. See if your expectations have changed. Here are the questions:

a. Would I work better in a large or a small organization?
b. How important is geographic location to me? To my family?
c. Do I work better alone or as a member of a group?
d. Am I a follower or a leader?
e. Do I think before I act?
f. Do I like working with people or with things?
g. Do I work well under pressure?
h. Do I have good ideas?
i. Do I listen well?
j. Do I make proper decisions?
k. Do I express myself well in writing and orally?
l. What do I admire in others?
m. What do I enjoy doing most?
n. What accomplishments have satisfied me most?
o. What are my shortcomings? What have I done to correct my shortcomings?
p. What do I want to be doing five years from now? Ten years from now?
q. What skills and knowledge do I need to achieve my five- and ten-year goals?

RESOURCES

www.seekingsuccess.com/articles/art167.php3 - an article on telephone interviews; includes a "quick tips" list.

www.worktree.com/tb/IN_telephone.cfm - an article on mastering the telephone interview; includes other employment-related resources as well.

http://jobsearch.about.com/cs/interviews/a/phoneinterview.htm - provides great tips on planning and preparing for a telephone interview.

www.best-job-interview.com/phone-interview-tips.html - tips on telephone interviews and other job-specific interview tips as well.

TOP TEN INTERVIEW QUESTIONS

Preparing for an interview is important. According to Carole Martin, Monster.com contributing writer, too many job seekers stumble through interviews as if the questions are coming out of left field. But many interview questions can be expected! Study this list of the top ten interview questions and plan your answers before the interview so you can deliver them with confidence. Use the tips provided for each question in formulating your answers.

1. **What are your weaknesses?**
   This is the most dreaded question of all. Handle it by <u>minimizing your weakness</u> and emphasizing your strengths. *Stay away from personal qualities and concentrate on professional traits:* "I am always working on improving my communication skills to be a more effective presenter. I recently joined Toastmasters, which I find very helpful."

2. **Why should we hire you?**
   <u>Summarize your experiences</u>: "With five years' experience working in the financial industry and my proven record of saving the company money, I could make a big difference in your company. I'm confident I would be a great addition to your team."

3. **Why do you want to work here?**
   The interviewer is listening for an <u>answer</u> that indicates you've given this some thought and are not sending out résumés just because there is an opening. For example, "I've selected key companies whose mission statements are in line with my values, where I know I could be excited about what the company does, and this company is very high on my list of desirable choices."

4. **What are your goals?**
   Sometimes it's best to talk about <u>short-term and intermediate goals</u> rather than locking yourself into the distant future. For example, "My immediate goal is to get a job in a growth-oriented company. My long-term goal will depend on where the company goes. I hope to eventually grow into a position of responsibility."

5. **Why did you leave (or why are you leaving) your job?**
   If you're unemployed, state your reason for leaving in a positive context: "I managed to survive two rounds of corporate downsizing, but the third round was a 20 percent reduction in the workforce, which included me."

   If you are employed, focus on what you want in your next job: "After two years, I made the decision to look for a company that is team-focused, where I can add my experience."

6. **When were you most satisfied in your job?**
   The interviewer wants to know what <u>motivates you</u>. If you can relate an example of a job or project when you were excited, the interviewer will get an idea of your preferences. "I was very satisfied in my last job because I worked directly with the customers and their problems; that is an important part of the job for me."

7. **What can you do for us that other candidates can't?**

   What makes you unique? This will take an assessment of your experiences, skills, and traits. Summarize concisely: "I have a unique combination of strong technical skills, and the ability to build strong customer relationships. This allows me to use my knowledge and break down information to be more user-friendly."

8. **What are three positive things your last boss would say about you?**

   It's time to pull out your old performance appraisals and boss's quotes. This is a great way to brag about yourself through someone else's words: "My boss has told me that I am the best designer he has ever had. He knows he can rely on me, and he likes my sense of humor."

9. **What salary are you seeking?**

   It is to your advantage if the employer tells you the range first. <u>Prepare</u> by knowing the going rate in your area, and your bottom line or walk-away point. One possible answer would be: "I am sure when the time comes, we can agree on a reasonable amount. In what range do you typically pay someone with my background?"

10. **If you were an animal, which one would you want to be?**

    Interviewers use this type of psychological question to see if you can think quickly. If you answer "a bunny," you will make a soft, passive impression. If you answer "a lion," you will be seen as aggressive. What type of personality would it take to get the job done? What impression do you want to make?

COMMON (Traditional) INTERVIEW QUESTIONS
-Behavioral interview questions are on page 66

Read through the following lists of common interview questions. Some of the questions (or very similar ones) are on more than one list. Select one list to outline your response to each question as part of the Capstone Project for this unit.

LIST 1:

The following lists of interview questions are considered some of the most commonly asked interview questions.

1. Why do you want to work for us?

2. Why should we hire you?

3. What can you tell me about yourself?

4. What are your strongest (or weakest) personal qualities?

5. What do you expect to be doing in ten years?

6. Do you prefer working with others or by yourself?

7. Have you ever changed your major during your education? Why?

8. What have been your most rewarding or disappointing work (or school) experiences?

9. Have you established any new goals lately?

10. What are your long- and short-term goals?

11. What were your best and worst subjects in college?

12. What sort of jobs did you have while you were in college?

13. What makes you happiest at work?

COMMON (Traditional) INTERVIEW QUESTIONS
LIST 2:

1. Tell me about yourself.

2. What do you know about our company?

3. Why do you want to work for us?

4. What unique qualities or abilities would you bring this job?

5. What are your major strengths and weaknesses?

6. How long do you plan to stay at our company?

7. Where do you see yourself in five years?

8. Tell me about a time that you failed at something, and what you did afterwards.

9. What do you do in your spare time?

10. Describe a time when you worked on a team project. What was your relative position on the team? Were you satisfied with your contribution? How could it have been better?

11. Why did you choose your school and course of study?

12. Think back to a situation in which a conflict existed. Tell me how you resolved that conflict.

13. Tell me about a project that you completed. Describe in detail how you managed it and describe the outcome.

14. What salary are you expecting?

15. What other types of jobs or companies are you considering?

COMMON (Traditional) INTERVIEW QUESTIONS
LIST 3:

1. Describe the characteristics of an individual whom you especially admire.

2. What is important to you in a job?

3. What do you think determines a person's progress in an organization?

4. Describe something you've done that shows initiative and willingness to work.

5. Describe a time when you worked well under pressure.

6. Describe a time when you worked effectively with others.

7. Describe a time when you organized a major project.

8. Describe a time when you motivated and led others.

9. Describe a time when you solved a difficult problem.

10. Describe a time when you accepted constructive criticism.

11. What position do you plan to have in five years?

12. What are your greatest strengths?

13. When did you choose your college major and what are some of the factors that led you to choose your major?

14. What are some of the factors that led you to choose the university you attended?

COMMON (Traditional) INTERVIEW QUESTIONS
LIST 4:

1. Tell us about yourself.

2. What are your career plans (long term and short term)? What position do you plan to have in five years?

3. What are some of the factors that led you to choose your college major? Your college/university? When did you choose your college major?

4. What courses did you like least? Best? Explain.

5. What do you know about opportunities in the field in which you are trained?

6. What do you know about our company? Why do you want to work for us?

7. Why should we hire you? What qualifications do you have that make you feel that you should be hired over others?

8. What do you consider your greatest strengths and/or weaknesses?

9. What do you think determines a person's progress in an organization?

10. How do your qualifications compare with the job requirements?

11. Describe a time when you (a) worked well under pressure, (b) worked effectively with others, (c) organized a major project, (d) motivated and led others, (e) solved a difficult problem, and (f) accepted constructive criticism.

12. Describe something you have done that shows initiative and willingness to work.

13. How have your extracurricular activities, part-time work experience, and/or volunteer work prepared you for work in our company?

14. What is important to you in a job? What interests you most about this job?

15. What are your salary expectations?

16. Describe the characteristics of an individual whom you especially admire.

17. Are you willing to take some psychological or drug tests?

SELECTED BEHAVIORAL INTERVIEW QUESTIONS
LIST 5:

Behavioral interview questions are ones that make you think through a situation and give a careful, well-planned answer to the question. As explained on page 45, use the BAR method to structure your answers in three parts: "B" – background; "A" – action; and "R" – results. *Here are a few examples of behavioral interview questions that you should prepare for before your interview:

1. How have you demonstrated initiative in the past six months?

2. Think about a difficult boss, professor, or other person. What made him or her difficult? How did you successfully interact with this person?

3. Think about a complex project or assignment you have been given. What approach did you take to complete the project or assignment?

4. Tell me about an occasion where you needed to work with a group to get a job done.

5. Tell me about a time when you worked with a person who did things very differently from you. How did you get the job done?

6. Describe your two or three greatest accomplishments to date.

7. Tell me about a challenge that you successfully met.

8. What leadership positions have you held? Describe your leadership style.

9. Summarize a situation where you successfully persuaded others to do something or to see your point of view.

10. What new ideas or suggestions have you generated while at school or work?

11. Describe a situation where class assignments and work or personal   activities conflicted. How did you prioritize? How did you manage your time? What was the outcome?

12. Tell me about a complex problem you solved. Describe the process you used.

*Additional sample behavioral interview questions can be found at Quintessential Careers website. Check out their 150 interview questions database for samples of both traditional and behavioral interview questions and excellent sample responses: http://www.quintcareers.com/interview_question_database/.

According to a human resources professional for one of Michigan's largest employers, the following questions are asked of all interviewees at this company:

1. With what teamwork activities have you been involved?

2. How did you deal with confrontation with this team?

3. How did you facilitate change and deal with others in the team who had a different point of view or opinion than you?

Unit II - Oral Communication

Capstone Project for Unit II - Oral Communication

The Capstone Project for Unit II is designed to apply the main topics in this unit into one integrated activity. This project consists of an individual component and a team component. You will experience each step of preparing and giving an oral presentation, including a self-assessment component. The integration of the unit topics via the completion of the activities in this project will increase your understanding of effective communication, including interpersonal communication within a team setting while improving your oral communication skills.

Instructions for Unit II Capstone Project individual component:

1. Prepare an outline of an oral presentation to inform (3 minutes in length is recommended) following the "golden rule of public speaking" as explained in this unit.

2. Complete a *related factors report* (based on the four related factors explained on page 80.)

3. Design an effective visual aid designed to use in your oral presentation.

4. Deliver your oral presentation to inform with a visual aid in class, which will be videotaped.

5. Complete the *video feedback self-evaluation* after reviewing the video of your presentation (self-evaluation questions provided on page 87.)

6. Utilize the topics in Unit II to complete these activities.

Instructions for Unit II Capstone Project <u>team component</u>:

1. Form teams according to your instructors directions. As a team, compile a *team oral communication resource file* that includes resources and information on the following topics:
   a. Giving effective presentations
   b. Designing effective visual aids
   c. Effective teams and teambuilding issues
   d. Intercultural communications

2. When you have completed your *team oral communication resource file*, each team will give a 10-15 minute oral presentation to inform based on your findings. Your purpose is to inform the rest of the class about the resources and information your team found for each topic <u>or</u> your instructor may assign one topic per team to give their presentation on. Check with your instructor for specific directions.

3. Prepare an outline of your team presentation (follow the "golden rule" as explained on page 85) and design appropriate visual aids.

4. Utilize the topics in Unit II to complete these activities.

✓ **Resource for students to prepare for Unit II assignments:**
   Go to www.ThinkOutsideTheSlide.com to sign up for the "Seven Day PowerPoint E-Course". You will receive seven PowerPoint lessons via email. These lessons will provide you with valuable tips on effective slide design, good structure, creating a clear message, and how to include photos and graphs in your slideshows.

TOPIC	**Communication Process – Verbal Communication**
DEFINITION	**Verbal communication** is the process of sending and receiving messages with words. It consists of the spoken words we use to communicate, including the way we speak (phrasing, rate of speech, and voice level.)
RATIONALE	Effective communication is truly an art form. Much of the research on identifying those skills most important for success in the workplace, find effective communication skills to be at the top of the list. Recruiters report that effective communication skills are most desirable in applicants, referring to both written and oral communication skills. Those individuals who represent the top ranks of nearly every organization often attribute their ability to communicate effectively to their success.

KEY POINTS

1. The communication process consists of a message being sent and received. The communication process consists of three elements:
   - verbal communication
   - nonverbal communication
   - listening

   Remember that verbal communication makes up only one-third of the communication process. Anyone who strives to become a great communicator must focus on developing their skills and abilities in all three elements of the communication process. The remaining two elements of the communication process (nonverbal communication and listening) are discussed in the following sections on pages 72 and 75

2. The need for effective communication skills is more important in today's workplace than ever. Technology has added to the complexities of public speaking and the skill set needed to deliver effective presentations. Check out these public speaking tips from Toastmasters International (http://www.toastmasters.org):
   a. know the room
   b. know the audience
   c. know your material
   d. relax
   e. visualize yourself giving your speech
   f. realize that people want you to succeed
   g. do not apologize
   h. concentrate on the message—not the medium

      i.   turn nervousness into positive energy

      j.   gain experience

ACTIVITIES

1. Find an online resource that discusses ways you can improve your verbal communication skills. Prepare a one-page summary of the major points. Be prepared to discuss what you learned in class.

2. First make a list of five skills and/or attributes that you feel contribute most to effective verbal communication. Next, form a team with 3-4 of your classmates. Compare and discuss your lists. You'll need to compile one list of five skills and/or attributes for your team. Your instructor will ask each team to share their list with the rest of the class and record their list on the board. Have a class discussion to compare the five skills and/or abilities identified by each team. As a class, discuss why these skills and/or attributes are important for effective verbal communication.

TOPIC	**Communication Process – Nonverbal Communication**

DEFINITION	**Nonverbal communication** consists of the unspoken signs we communicate with through our body language, facial expressions, eye contact, gestures, touch, appearance, space, and time.

RATIONALE	Research shows that "how" something is said (nonverbal communication) is much more powerful than "what" is actually said (verbal communication.) According to a UCLA study, as much as <u>93 percent</u> of communication effectiveness is determined by nonverbal cues. In addition, consider these findings related to what factors contribute to the *impact* of a presentation:

- 7 percent determined by the words used
- 38 percent by voice quality
- 55 percent by the nonverbal communication

Read more about this research at:
http://humanresources.about.com/od/interpersonalcommunicatio1/a/nonverbal_com.htm.

KEY POINTS	

1. The communication process consists of three elements:
   - verbal communication
   - nonverbal communication
   - listening

   Remember that nonverbal communication makes up only one-third of the communication process. Anyone who strives to become a great communicator must focus on developing their skills and abilities in all three elements of the communication process. The remaining element of the communication process (listening) is discussed in the next section on page 75.

2. Research shows that when verbal and nonverbal cues conflict, people will determine meaning from the nonverbal cues.
   a. 55 percent of the first impact you have is nonverbal; 33 percent is the way you use your voice, and 12 percent is the actual words you say.

3. Meanings of nonverbal communication are determined by and can vary between the different cultural group(s) you belong to. This is why nonverbal cues are considered culture bound.
   a. Assigned meanings can vary greatly between different individuals and groups.
   b. You may belong to multiple cultural groups of various sizes through membership in an ethnic group, your

72

family, your profession, your social group, and other groups.

4. Nonverbal communication is multi-sensory (sight, smell, touch/feel, taste, and hearing.)

5. Nonverbal communication is often ambiguous since interpretation of these attributes can vary greatly between individuals, genders, and especially cultures. The different types of nonverbal behaviors include:
   a. eye contact
   b. facial expressions
   c. gestures
   d. posture and body orientation
   e. touch
   f. proximity
   g. vocal elements (nonverbal speech sounds such as tone, pitch, volume, inflection, rhythm, and pace); remember, it's not what you say but *how* you say it.

6. To improve nonverbal communication skills, understand and apply the following techniques:
   a. maintain eye contact with the listener (see special section on improving your eye communication on page 76.)
   b. utilize the power of smiling; it communicates many positive feelings such as warmth, friendliness, and approval
   c. reduce or eliminate physical barriers
   d. probe for more information
   e. be wary of assigning nonverbal meanings out of context
   f. associate with people from diverse cultures
   g. observe yourself on video tape occasionally

ACTIVITIES

1. Test your nonverbal communication skills with this activity: first, find someone in your class whose birthday is the same month as yours <u>without</u> speaking; second, find someone in your class who has the same color car as yours <u>without</u> speaking.

2. Find an online resource that discusses ways you can improve your nonverbal communication skills. Prepare a one-page summary of the major points. Be prepared to discuss what you learned in class.

3. Watch this 30-second YouTube video on the Top Ten Positive Gestures:
www.youtube.com/watch?v=BmU5MO7ZaZU&NR=1.

4. Watch this 26-second YouTube video on The Power of Nonverbal Communications:
www.youtube.com/watch?v=cS1LI_ut3fs&feature=related.

RESOURCES

www3.usal.es/~nonverbal/introduction.htm - provides a list of links to resources related to nonverbal communication including links to research websites, papers, abstracts, and journals on this topic.

http://humanresources.about.com/od/interpersonalcommunicatio1/a/nonverbal_com.htm - learn more about nonverbal communication and take nonverbal communication interpretation quizzes on different aspects of nonverbal communication.

TOPIC	**Communication Process – Listening**

DEFINITION

Listening is a conscious process and is more than just hearing. Listening is the conscious effort to understand and analyze what is being spoken. Most people are very inefficient listeners due to a variety of barriers to listening that constantly challenge our focus.

RATIONALE

Effective communication is truly an art form. Much of the research on identifying those skills most important for success in the workplace, find effective communication skills to be at the top of the list. Recruiters report that effective communication skills are most desirable in applicants, referring to both written and oral communication skills. All of this leads to the reality that those individuals who represent the top ranks of nearly every organization often attribute their ability to communicate effectively to their success.

KEY POINTS

1. The communication process consists of three elements:
    - verbal communication
    - nonverbal communication
    - listening

    Remember that listening makes up only one-third of the communication process. Anyone who strives to become a great communicator must focus on developing their skills and abilities in all three elements of the communication process as discussed in the previous two sections.

2. Numerous mental and physical barriers distract and compete for our attention and prevent us from listening effectively, such as noise, our state of mind, the time of day, and much more. Apply the items from the following checklist for improving your listening:
    a. Talk less; listen more. Concentrate on what the speaker is saying.
    b. Block out distracting thoughts.
    c. Turn off the TV; shut the window; remove all distractions.
    d. Be tolerant of all speakers.
    e. Paraphrase the speaker's ideas by silently repeating the message; summarize the ideas in your own words silently.
    f. Observe nonverbal cues. What is the speaker really saying?

3. Be aware of the barriers that make it difficult for you to listen effectively and efficiently (mental and physical barriers.)
   a. Learn to improve your focus for better listening by eliminating or learning to ignore barriers.

4. The average person listens very inefficiently, not hearing and processing as much as 75 percent of what is spoken.
   a. The best communicators are excellent listeners.
   b. Practice is necessary to be an efficient listener.

5. Improve your eye communication will improve your listening.
   a. Your eyes are the only part of your central nervous system that directly connect with another person. In the business world, you use your eyes to communicate 90 percent of the time in face-to-face conversations.

6. Remember the three "I's" of eye communication:
   a. intimacy
   b. intimidation
   c. involvement

   In the business world, involvement is most appropriate and effective. Communication expert Bert Decker explains that intimacy and intimidation are both communicated by looking at a person for an extended period of time (10 seconds to a minute or more.) Involvement is communicated by looking at someone for shorter periods of time (less than 10 seconds) before looking away. Anything more becomes intimacy or intimidation; anything less may be interpreted as untrustworthy.

7. Remember these eye communication tips:
   - Avoid darting eyes (what we tend to do when we're nervous.)
   - Darting eyes undermine your credibility.
   - Look directly at a person and hold eye contact for several seconds at a time.
   - You can develop the five second habit with practice.
   - Observe how others use eye contact and notice what makes you feel comfortable and uncomfortable.

ACTIVITIES

1. Test your listening skills by playing the grapevine game. One person starts by whispering a short message (1-2 sentences) into another person's ear.

a. The second person then passes the message on to the third person, then to the fourth person, and so on.

b. When the last person receives the message he or she tells the entire class what the message was they heard; then the first person in the grapevine tells what the message was originally.

c. Compare the messages… how good were your listening skills?

2. Find an online resource that discusses ways you can improve your listening skills. Prepare a one-page summary of the major points. Be prepared to discuss what you learned in class.

3. Form teams of 3-5 students. Brainstorm as a team and list as many barriers you can that prevent people from being good listeners.

a. Categorize your list of barriers as either *mental* or *physical*.

b. Discuss what the most common barriers are for each team member and identify ways you can eliminate or learn to ignore these barriers.

c. When completed with your team's list, check your list against the list of common communication barriers provided at: www.nsba.org/sbot/toolkit/CommStyl.html.

RESOURCES

www.d.umn.edu/student/loon/acad/strat/ss_listening.html - provides strategies for students to improve their listening skills.

www.wittcom.com/listening_quiz.htm - complete this online listening quiz and learn more about improving your listening skills.

TOPIC   **Oral Presentations**

DEFINITION   There are three basic types of oral presentations:
- a. Informative
- b. Persuasive
- c. Entertaining

KEY POINTS   1. Utilize the three "P's" for effective presentation skills:
- a. preparation
- b. practice
- c. performance

Nothing can take the place of great preparation followed by plenty of practice to lead to a great performance. Confidence comes from a strong sense of being well prepared. Think of a time when you did a great job in a presentation and you'll recall the work you put in planning and preparing. Effective presentations are well planned, well organized, and well delivered.

2. Because communication skills are consistently ranked as the #1 skill for success by top executives, presentation skills are equally important. The more you advance in an organization, the more likely effective presentation skills will be required.

3. Your most important tool for an effective presentation is an outline that enables you to plan, organize, and deliver effectively.

4. Your outline should follow the "golden rule" of public speaking (see template page 85 and example outline page 86):
- a. Tell them what you're going to say
- b. Say it
- c. Tell them what you said

5. The most important factor to increase the success of an oral presentation is <u>practice</u>.
- a. The only way to improve your skills is to gain experience by giving oral presentations.
- b. A major obstacle in improving presentation skills is the lack of awareness of how bad you really are.

6. Speak from an outline that follows the "golden rule" of oral presentations (see template and example pages 85-86.)
- a. Print your outline on standard sized paper (no index cards.)

    b. Use a larger font size if it helps you to better follow your outline when speaking.

7. Do not forget the impact of nonverbal communication on your oral presentation. Nonverbal communication can enhance or detract from your presentation.
    a. Effective use of eye contact makes you appear credible and confident to your audience.
    b. Showing enthusiasm and passion for what you're talking about is a major contributor to the effectiveness of any presentation.
    c. Use appropriate gestures and body language.

STEPS

1. Identify the topic and purpose (to inform, persuade, or entertain) of your oral presentation.

2. Research your topic as necessary.

3. Check out each of the *related factors* that directly affect your presentation:
    a. <u>Time factor</u> – first, you must find out the amount of time you are expected to speak before you can prepare your presentation.
    b. <u>Audience factor</u> – know the makeup of your audience; the audience is crucial in determining the tone of your presentation and in determining the appropriate level of vocabulary and technical terms.
    c. <u>Room factor</u> – know the size of the room you'll be speaking in, the type of seating and room arrangement, the speaker's platform or podium arrangement, and be familiar with any technical equipment you'll be using (microphone, computer, remote control.)
    d. <u>Scheduling factor</u> – find out what time of the day you are speaking and the placement of your presentation among other presenters. Scheduling factors can make a difference in the mood of your audience, their attention span, and their ability to focus.

4. Outline your presentation following the "golden rule" of oral presentations (see example outline on page 85.)
    a. Outline the "introduction" including an attention getter and introduction of your main points.
    b. Outline the "body" of your presentation by outlining each of your major points, providing adequate support for each. Remember to <u>not</u> use complete sentences in

your outline. This will prevent you from reading your presentation to your audience.

    c. Outline the "summary" of your presentation by re-stating your main points and if appropriate, asking for questions.

5. Prepare at least one visual aid that <u>enhances</u> your presentation as outlined in the "Guidelines for Visual Aids" topic beginning on page 88.

6. Once you're well prepared, you must practice, practice, practice.

ACTIVITIES

1. Impromptu speaking activity—everyone needs to bring an item in a paper bag to class without telling anyone what your item is. Be sure to be familiar with the "golden rule" for oral presentations on page 85.
       a. Optional – conduct peer evaluations as part of this activity by having three students evaluate each speaker.
       b. Utilize the "golden rule" approach for this activity.
       c. All students place their bagged item on a table when they come into class.
       d. To begin, one student will select a bagged item and step out into the hall to prepare. Each student will have two minutes to prepare outside the classroom while one student is giving their presentation. Once the first student is giving their presentation, another student is always "on-deck" in the hall preparing. This procedure allows each student about two minutes to prepare.
       e. Remember to follow the "golden rule" of oral presentations and you will be able to give a much more organized and effective presentation. ***Hint***: Start with an introduction of yourself, your topic (whatever your item is) and some kind of attention getter; then pick two to three major points you want to discuss about the item, *e.g.,* three uses of the item); then conclude by re-stating your major points!

2. Prepare an outline following the "golden rule" based on a topic you choose for a three-minute oral presentation to inform (part of the Capstone Project for this unit.)

81

3. Check out the *related* factors (as explained in this topic on page 80 and listed below) that will affect your oral presentation to inform as assigned in Activity 2 (part of the Capstone Project for this unit.)
    a. Prepare your *report of related factors* for the four related factors listed below.
    b. Discuss the implications of each factor and how each factor affects your planning, preparation, and presentation:
        1) Time factor
        2) Audience factor
        3) Room factor
        4) Scheduling factor

4. Videotape yourself giving an oral presentation according to your instructor's directions (part of the Capstone Project for this unit.)
    a. Prepare your *video feedback self-evaluation* by viewing your videotaped oral presentation and answering the questions on page 87 (part of the Capstone Project for this unit.)
    b. Refer to the following *elements of effective oral presentations checklist* on page 84 to help you complete this activity.
    c. Check with your instructor for format requirements and any other instructions for completing this activity.

5. Meet with your teammates to begin compiling your *team oral communication resource file* (part of the Capstone Project for this unit.)
    a. Visit websites that provide information on giving effective presentations and printout information from these websites to include in your team's resource file or as directed by your instructor.

RESOURCES

Effective presentations website designed to provide many links, resources, and online tutorials for the improvement of oral presentation skills - www.kumc.edu/SAH/OTEd/jradel/effective.html

Presentation Helper website for designing effective visual presentations, includes "the seven deadly sins of visual presentations" - www.presentationhelper.co.uk/7sinsvisual.htm

Presentation Helper website focusing on the power of visual information www.presentationmagazine.com/visual-communication-of-information853.htm

Website for Toastmasters International includes "10 Tips for Successful Public Speaking"- www.toastmasters.org/tips.asp

Small business website offers business tips on giving effective PowerPoint presentations - http://sbinfocanada.about.com/cs/management/qt/powerptpres.htm

Elements of Effective Oral Presentations Checklist

Note: The following is an example of an oral presentations checklist. Use this list when you prepare a presentation or when you listen to someone else giving a presentation.

_____ Effective use of eye contact

_____ Well prepared; meets time requirements

_____ Content is well organized, logical

_____ Effective use of visual aids

_____ Well-designed visual aids

_____ Uses appropriate volume and rate of speech

_____ Uses natural speaking voice

_____ Confident, relaxed appearance

_____ Uses effective phrasing and emphasis

_____ Avoids distracting gestures

_____ Uses proper tone

_____ Exhibits enthusiasm/passion for the subject matter

_____ Avoids use of filler words

_____ Uses appropriate level of vocabulary for audience

Golden Rule for Oral Presentations

(1) Tell them what you're going to say
(2) Say it
(3) Tell them what you said

ORAL PRESENTATION OUTLINE TEMPLATE

Follow this format for planning and delivering a well-organized oral presentation that follows the "golden rule":

> An attention getter can be asking a question or stating an impressive fact or startling statistic

I. Introduction (tell them what you're going to say)

   A. Introduce yourself

   B. Include an attention getter

   C. Introduce your topic

      1. Preview your main points #1 (tell them what you're going to say)

      2. Main point #2

      3. Main point #3

II. Body (say it)

   A. Main point #1

      1. Sub point (supporting information)

      2. Continue with any additional sub points as necessary

   B. Main point #2

      1. Sub point (supporting information)

      2. Continue with any additional sub points as necessary

   C. Main point #3

      1. Sub point (supporting information)

      2. Continue with any additional sub points as necessary

III. Summary (tell them what you said)

   A. Restate your main points (tell them what you said.)

   B. Ask for questions if appropriate

   C. Include a strong finish

TOPIC:　　The Amish Way of Life

PURPOSE: To inform

I.　Introduction
　　A. Welcome and introduce myself
　　B. Imagine life without TV
　　C. Amish way of life
　　　　1. Lifestyle
　　　　2. Clothing
　　　　3. Religion

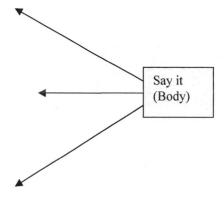

Tell them what
you're going
to say
(Introduction)

II.　Body
　　A. Lifestyle
　　　　1. No telephone
　　　　2. No electricity
　　　　3. Source of transportation
　　B. Clothing
　　　　1. Men's
　　　　　　a. Buttons only
　　　　　　b. Pants with suspenders
　　　　2. Women's
　　　　　　a. Dresses
　　　　　　b. Black cape/bonnet
　　　　3. Children's
　　　　　　a. Girls
　　　　　　b. Boys
　　C. Religion
　　　　1. Take turns with services
　　　　2. Big meal
　　　　3. Games

Say it
(Body)

III.　Summary
　　A. Lifestyle
　　B. Clothing
　　C. Religion

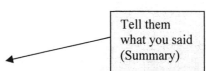

Tell them
what you said
(Summary)

86

Video Feedback Self-Evaluation Instructions and Questions for an Oral Presentation

(part of the Capstone Project for this unit)

Directions: Watch your videotaped oral presentation in its entirety several times when you have no distractions. Reflect on how you felt while you were giving your presentation. Read each of the questions below. Type your response to each of the following seven questions (be sure to number each of response):

1. What do you feel you did best?

2. What do you feel needs the most improvement? What can you do to improve on this factor the next time?

3. How did your audience react/respond during your presentation and how did this response make you feel?

4. If you were to give the same oral presentation again, what changes would you make to the content?

5. How well do you feel you did in preparing for each of the "related factors" listed below? -Refer to page 80 as needed for explanations of each "related factor" and specific points to discuss.
    -Time factor (too long, too short, under prepared)
    -Audience factor (interest in topic, appropriate vocabulary)
    -Room factor (seating arrangement, familiarity with equipment, movement in room, use of podium)
    -Scheduling factor (prepared for mood of audience, time of day and sequence among other speakers, and other barriers)
6. List two goals you have to further develop your oral presentation skills.

7. Rate your overall performance on a scale of 1-10 with "1" being lowest and "10" being highest.

Guidelines for Visual Aids – Including PowerPoint

1. Visual aids can increase the persuasiveness of a presentation, the comprehension by audience members, and the perception of the credibility and professionalism of the presenter. Research has found that 55 percent of the way people take in information during a presentation is visually (versus 38 percent vocally and 7 percent through text.)

2. Well-designed visual aids enhance a presentation, making it more interesting and making the presenter appear better prepared by audience members. The effective use of visual aids is more relevant today than ever before. Research has proven the power of visual information in creating a more memorable experience for your audience.

   A new approach in presentation software is Prezi, a "zooming presentation editor." This application is available free online at http://prezi.com/ and utilizes the power of visual information. You can create a visually based presentation including integrating video and pictures quickly and easily. Prezi is designed as an alternative to the use of PowerPoint with less emphasis on text and more emphasis on visuals.

3. A variety of visual aids may be used, such as:
   a. Objects, models
   b. Maps, graphs, charts
   c. Pictures (posters, photographs, drawings)
   d. Boards used to write on (chalkboard, whiteboard, flipcharts)
   e. Media items (films, video, audio recordings)
   f. Handouts
   g. Presentation technology like PowerPoint and Prezi -refer to the PowerPoint checklist on page 91

4. Basic rules for designing effective visual aids relate to <u>four</u> key issues:
   a. **Visibility** – minimum font sizes to use for handouts, transparencies, and slides vary (see chart below.)
   b. **Emphasis/content** – visual aids should compliment and enhance your presentation; do not try to put "everything" in your text-based visual aids; focus on relevance and simplicity in designing visual aids. For PowerPoint slides, follow the "Rule of 6s" as much as possible. Your goal is to have no more than six lines per slide and six words per line. Always use an outline

88

format for your slides (avoid complete sentences.) Remember that your slides should <u>not</u> be the focus of your presentation. If your audience is reading your slides, they're not listening to you.

   c. **Balance** – visuals should be appealing to your audience with well-balanced use of text, color, and/or graphics.

   d. **Color** – use appropriate colors so that your text-based visuals are not difficult to read; make sure your audience can see and read your visuals easily.

      1) Check the background colors for ease of readability given the light and size of the room in which you will be presenting.

      2) Be sure the font size is large enough and the color distinct so as not to blend in with the background. Recommended font sizes for handouts and PowerPoint slides are as follows:

	Handouts	Slides
Title:	14-18 pt.	42-48 pt.
Subtitles:	12-16 pt.	32-42 pt.
Body text:	12-14 pt.	28-32 pt.

5. Be sure to give visuals like slides and transparencies a test run in the room you will be presenting in or a similar environment to check for readability in the lighting your presentation will be viewed in and the room size.

   a. Will everyone be able to see and read your visuals, no matter where they are seated?

   b. Check that all hyperlinks in your slideshow are working.

6. Be sure to practice your presentation with your visual aids and any equipment, controls, and proper lighting.

   a. Do stand to the side of visual aids, never in front.

   b. Do use a pointing device if appropriate.

   c. Do not point at the screen when using transparencies or slides-- point at the transparency <u>on</u> the projector or point out something on a slide with the mouse or pointing device.

7. Know the placement of any visual aids within your presentation. Be sure to refer your audience to the visual by page number, using a pointing device, or whatever is appropriate.

   a. Distribute any handouts before or after your presentation, <u>not</u> during.

b. Do not display a visual until you need to refer to it.
c. Point out where the material you are discussing can be found in a handout.
d. Do remove a visual as soon as you have covered it.

ACTIVITIES

1. Visit websites that provide information on designing effective visuals to add to your team's *oral communication resource file* (part of the Capstone Project for this unit.)

2. Register for a free Prezi account online at http://prezi.com/. Learn how to use Prezi by completing the three "basic" Prezi lessons. Create a Prezi presentation on a topic of your choice and include a relevant YouTube video and picture in your presentation. Turn in a print out of just your "overview" page (page 1) by following the printing instructions provided at Prezi.com.

RESOURCES

Presentation Helper website focusing on the power of visual information www.presentationmagazine.com/visual-communication-of-information853.htm

Effective Presentations website provides resources, links, and online tutorials for designing effective presentations - www.kumc.edu/SAH/OTEd/jradel/effective.html

Presentation Helper website for designing effective visual presentations, includes "the seven deadly sins of visual presentations" - www.presentationhelper.co.uk/7sinsvisual.htm

Small Business Canada website offers business tips on "giving effective PowerPoint presentations" – http://sbinfocanada.about.com/library/biztips/bl_biztips_14.htm

PowerPoint Checklist:

____ 1. Use outline approach for slide content; <u>no</u> complete sentences; follow "Rule of 6s" on majority of slides (6 lines/slide, 6 words/line)

____ 2. Use informative title on each slide

____ 3. Introduces main points on slide 2

____ 4. Use sans serif fonts (like Arial); <u>not</u> serif fonts (like Times New Roman)

____ 5. Use contrasting color for slide background and text; dark background with light text or light background with dark text (e.g. antique gold or yellow is best contrast with dark blue)

____ 6. Titles text: (large enough/easy to read), e.g. 42-48 pt. font

____ 7. Subtitles text: (large enough/easy to read), e.g. 32-42 pt. font

____ 8. Body text: (large enough/easy to read), e.g. 28-32 pt. font

____ 9. Titles and subtitles – Capitalize first letter of significant words (Title Case)

____ 10. Body text of slides – left justified, capitalize only first letter of first word in each line and proper nouns (Sentence case)

____ 11. Bullets/numbers – used effectively; provides hierarchy as applicable; provides relationship/structure to content

____ 12. Graphics – use (relevant) pictures, not clip art; use appropriately for emphasis

____ 13. Include a summary slide at the end that lists your main points again

TOPIC	**Teams** (teamwork, teambuilding, communicating in teams)
DEFINITION	Webster defines the noun *team* as "a group of people working or playing together" and the verb *team* as "to join in cooperative activity."

Teamwork is the cooperative/collaborative effort by members of a group to achieve a common goal.

KEY POINTS

1. Being a team player and having experience working in teams are highly valued skills by employers today.

2. The use of teams in organizations continues to increase as teamwork replaces the traditional way of doing business.
   a. Organizations continue to move toward team-based decision-making rather than individual-based decisions because teams consistently <u>outperform</u> individuals.
   b. The use of teams enables an organization to better utilize their resources and provides greater flexibility.
   c. The collective experiences and judgment of a team combined with the wide variety of skills far exceeds the talents of one individual.

3. Essentials of the team process are teambuilding, teamwork, leadership, and communication to create a collaborative effort to achieve a common goal.

4. Four stages of team development exist: forming, storming, norming, and performing. Understanding this evolutionary process of team development will help you to be a better team member.

   Stage 1 – Forming
   Initial formation of team:
   a. characterized by uncertainty with polite and tentative communication
   b. conflict is avoided
   c. goals are unclear and member roles not yet assigned
   d. must allow conflict to develop to lead to Stage 2.

Stage 2 – Storming
Team defines itself:
- a. characterized by disagreement and competition among team members to clarify roles and goals
- b. trust begins when conflicts are resolved which leads to Stage 3

Stage 3 – Norming
Teamwork and commitment to the group develops:
- a. characterized by mutual trust and matching of skills with tasks
- b. constructive feedback is given within the team
- c. communication and cohesion develop which leads to Stage 4

Stage 4 - Performing
Full-fledged team develops:
- a. characterized by cooperation, with effective communication among members and a clear understanding of the team's goals
- b. team is functioning as a sum of its parts and not as individuals
- c. leadership functions shift and are distributed among members as appropriate

5. Conflict is a natural and necessary part of the team process.
   - a. "good" conflict is referred to as *cognitive* conflict.
   - b. cognitive conflict is constructive by focusing on issues (not people or personalities.)
   - c. conflict needs to occur to avoid groupthink.
   - d. "bad" conflict is referred to as *affective* conflict.
   - e. affective conflict is destructive because it focuses on people and personalities.

6. The best teams include the following characteristics:
   - a. 5-7 diverse members
   - b. commitment to common purpose, goals, and procedures (all team members know what needs to be done, when, by whom, how, why.)
   - c. mutual respect, trust, and support
   - d. open communication; listen and share ideas
   - e. shared leadership/shared responsibility
   - f. efficient, productive meetings (collaboration)
   - g. conflict resolution (respect differences in others)
   - h. utilization of member resources and talents

7. Be sure you play a positive role in your team:
   a. Do not withdraw during meetings; participate in the team process
   b. Good teams will vary leadership roles; leadership is emergent and not assigned
   c. Ask questions and get clarification
   d. Recognize the strengths and expertise each team member brings to the team process
   e. Do not compete with other team members; be willing to collaborate and recognize the talents of others
   f. Do not dominate discussion or ridicule ideas of others
   g. Contribute and complete your tasks as assigned
   h. Agree to disagree; consensus is crucial in a team; you won't always get your way

8. Research shows the top reasons the use of teams and the team process continues to increase in organizations are due to the following benefits:
   a. Better utilizes talents, time, and energy of employees
   b. Improves decision making and increases ownership of decisions
   c. Increases work capacity; more cost effective
   d. Increases employee morale

ACTIVITIES

1. Read more about teambuilding and related teambuilding issues. Check out the articles, resources, and links on a variety of teamwork related topics designed to help you develop an understanding of the team process.

2. Include printouts from the following websites in your team's oral communications resource file: http://teambuildinginc.com/ and http://leadership.monster.com/.

3. Form a team of three; prepare an outline for an oral presentation to inform (following the golden rule of oral presentations) on some aspect of leadership, teamwork, or teambuilding.

4. Understanding your own personality traits and leadership style will help you to understand your own behavior, especially in a team environment and how you fit with other personality types in your team. Complete one of the following online tests:
   a. Go to www.testcafe.com/lead/ to measure your leadership skills. Print out your test results to share in a class discussion.
   b. Complete the Jung-Meyers-Briggs typology test online at http://www.humanmetrics.com/ (click on "Jung typology test".) Print out your test results and the explanations about your personality type provided. Read about the other types so you have a better understanding of how differences in personality types affect our behavior and team dynamics.

5. Form a team with other classmates. Brainstorm ways to overcome team conflict and record your ideas. Next have each team member read this article at http://career-advice.monster.com/in-the-office/workplace -issues/overcome-team-conflict/article.aspx about overcoming team conflict. Compare your team's list with the suggestions in this article and discuss with your team.

6. Listen to this interview at www.thisamericanlife.org/radio-archives/episode/370/ruining-it-for-the-rest-of-us about how a researcher discovered that "one bad apple" on a team can spoil it for the rest of us. The research was conducted in college classrooms. Be prepared to discuss the different types of bad apple behaviors and how to prevent bad apples from ruining your team in class.

Teamwork Memo Assignment

Choose three quotes or proverbs that are most meaningful to you from the list of *Teamwork Quotes and Proverbs* found at www.heartquotes.net/teamwork-quotes.html or from a list provided by your instructor.

Prepare your response to these quotes in a memo using block format and the **OABC** framework for business writing. You can read more about this approach to business writing at www.allbusiness.com/finance-insurance/854596-1.html. Rank the three quotes or proverbs you choose in order of importance and explain what they mean to you in the body of your memo.

Your memo should have an **opening** (introductory) paragraph followed by an **agenda** (a preview of the main points to be covered.) After the agenda, write the **body** of your memo by discussing what each of the three quotes or proverbs you selected mean to you in a separate paragraph. Complete your memo with the **closing** section of your message. The content of the closing section can vary depending on the topic. For this assignment, a summary of your key points would be most relevant.

Your memo will have a minimum of six paragraphs, consisting of the following:
- one paragraph each for the opening, agenda, and closing
- three paragraphs for the body of your memo (one paragraph for each of the quotes or proverbs)

Be sure to use proper memo format as shown on page 117. Write the memo to your instructor and include an appropriate subject line. Initial your memo at your name before turning it in.

TOPIC	**Intercultural Communication**
	(refer to Unit III, pages 148-149 also)

DEFINITION Intercultural communication deals with understanding how people from different countries and cultures behave, communicate, and perceive the world around them. It also relates to the business world in dealing with and creating relationships between people from different cultures within a business or in conducting business across cultures.

BACKGROUND Communicating with other people and other cultures both orally and in writing will be one of your tasks in the global office. Communicating with people from other cultures requires that you know a bit about "context". People from *high-context* countries, like the Japanese and other Asians, seem vague when communicating. People in high-context countries use personal relationships as a way of doing business. People from high-context countries depend more on *how* you say or write something than on *what* you actually said or wrote. Speak or write to people in high-context countries using the *indirect* approach.

People from *low-context* countries, such as Germany, Holland, and many of the European countries, get right to the point in their oral and written communications. These people may seem rude, but they are not. Being brief and concise is the way they have learned to communicate over the years. Speak or write to people in low-context countries using the *direct* approach.

KEY POINTS

1. Determine whether the person you are writing or speaking to comes from a high- or low-context country.
    a. You can find this information by using the Internet or by going to your library.

2. Use expressions that are easily understood by people from other countries and other cultures.
    a. Avoid *idioms, clichés, slang, jargon, redundancies,* and *euphemisms;* avoid using contractions (an international person may not understand that the word "*won't,"* for instance, is a shortened form of *will not.)*

3. Use short, simple sentences and short paragraphs.

4. Avoid discussing controversial items, such as war, poverty, politics, and the like.

5. Use a traditional format for letters; the block style letter is easily interpreted by people from other cultures.
   a. If you are interested in how people from a certain culture or country format their letters, you can contact your local United States Post Office for information about international formats.

6. Use graphics or pictures whenever possible to help get your point across.

7. Strive for clarity in both oral and written presentations.

8. Use correct grammar and punctuation.

9. Learn some simple foreign phrases and include one or two of them in your oral or written presentation.

10. Speak slowly and clearly.

11. Listen without interrupting when you are speaking to someone from another culture or another country.

12. Smile; be pleasant when speaking with international people.

13. Always remember, the meanings of nonverbal communication are culturally determined.
    a. Common forms of nonverbal communication such as eye contact, smiling, and a wave of your hand mean distinctly different things in different cultures.

ACTIVITIES

1. Consult the Internet to get a list of idioms, clichés, slang, redundancies, and jargon.
   a. Prepare a short memo report summarizing and giving examples of what you have found (refer to Unit III, pages 116-117 for memo report format guidelines.)

2. Meet with your teammates to complete your *team oral communication resource file* (part of the Capstone Project for this unit.)
   a. Visit websites that provide information on intercultural communications and printout information from these websites to include in your team's resource file.

3. Checkout issues related to cultural differences at
   www.worldbiz.com/index.php.

4. Prepare an outline for a short oral presentation to report on a
   topic you or your instructor chooses for an audience from a
   high-context country.
   a. Give your oral presentation to the rest of your team
      members.
   b. Re-do the outline for an audience from a low-context
      country.
   c. Discuss what changes were made to adapt your
      presentations to the different audiences in your team or
      as a class.
   d. Turn in a copy of each outline as part of your Capstone
      Project for this unit.

5. Interview an international student or friend from another
   culture. Ask a minimum of the following seven questions and
   prepare a memo or presentation to share what you learned:
   a. How do the people of your country perceive
      Americans?
   b. What are some of your positive impressions of the
      United States?
   c. What are some of your negative impressions of the
      United States?
   d. What was the most difficult adjustment you had to
      make when you moved to this country?
   e. What are some communication barriers you
      encountered in this country?
   f. What are the most significant cultural differences you
      encountered in this country?
   g. What advice would you give to me if I were going to go
      to your country to live and work?

RESOURCES

www.kwintessential.co.uk/resources/culture-tests.html - a great
website to improve your intercultural communication skills;
provides information and resources related to cultural awareness
training and intercultural training; includes online quizzes to test
your skills.

http://cyborlink.com/ – the web's leading resource for international
business etiquette and manners.

www.culture-at-work.com/highlow.html - information on communicating across cultures with an emphasis on high and low context cultures.

http://ezinearticles.com/?Ten-Tips-for-Cross-Cultural-Communication&id=2196 – 10 tips for improving cross cultural communication.

Chaney, L. and J. Martin. *International Business Communication, 2nd edition.* Upper Saddle River, NJ: Prentice Hall, 2000.

Neuliep, J. W. *Intercultural Communication: A Contextual Approach.* New York: Houghton Mifflin, 2000.

Reynolds, Sara and Deborah Valentine. *Guide to Cross-Cultural Communication.* Upper Saddle River, NJ: Prentice Hall, 2004.

Victor, David. *International Business Communication.* New York: HarperCollins, 2002.

Unit III - Written Communication

Capstone Project for Unit III - Written Communication

The Capstone Project for Unit III is designed to apply the main topics in this unit into one integrated assignment. The integration of the unit topics via the completed assignments will result in a resource file that contains examples of common business documents. You will work in teams (your instructor will decide the number in each team) to complete the following collaborative projects. Your instructor will determine which of the following items to include in this project:

1. Form teams and <u>elect</u> someone in your team to act as facilitator. The other members of the team are project members. The facilitator will keep the team on task. Exchange email addresses and cell phone numbers. Create a cover page with your company name and team member names.

2. Design a <u>company letterhead</u> for use in a fictitious company you have organized within your group. Include a graphic for your company logo.

3. Design a <u>product</u> that your company will produce or a <u>service</u> your company will provide. Prepare a <u>memo</u> that includes a description of the product or service after your team has come to a final decision. Input is expected from all team members. Include information to answer the questions in the memo to your instructor:
   a. Who will use the product (the audience)?
   b. How does the product work?
   c. From what materials is the product made?
   d. What are the product's superior features in design and construction?
   e. What is the price? Is the price competitive?
   f. What kind of servicing will the product require?
   g. Are similar products available? If so, how does the product stack up against the competition?

4. Prepare a <u>brochure</u> (3-column, tri-fold) that promotes your product to consumers. Refer to the following articles to learn more about creating effective brochures and how to use effective brochure marketing:

   http://smallbusiness.yahoo.com/r-article-a-112337-m-6-sc-43-create_the_best_brochure-i http://marketing.about.com/od/directmarketin1/a/brochmktg.htm for tips and resources

5. Prepare a one-page <u>flyer</u> for a bulletin board or similar use for your company's product or service. Use both text and graphics. Use the A-I-D-A approach explained in this unit. Refer to www.tightwadmarketing.com/flyer.htm for tips on improving your flyer.

6. Prepare a <u>persuasive sales letter</u> to introduce your new product or service. The letter will be mailed or emailed to thousands of potential customers. Use the A-I-D-A approach.

7. During the time you are working on this project, your instructor will ask you to prepare a <u>progress report</u> on the status of your project.

8. Prepare a <u>press release</u> to announce the availability of your new product.

9. Prepare an <u>outline</u> for an oral presentation to inform or persuade. Your instructor will provide the time frame and more details about when you will give this presentation in class.

10. Prepare a <u>one-sided business card</u> for each team member. Your business card should include your name, the company name, address, and other information.

11. Give a <u>team presentation</u> of your product or service utilizing appropriate visual aids. Your instructor will assign the time frame.

12. Prepare an <u>executive summary</u> describing your project for your instructor.

13. Complete <u>peer evaluations</u> for the other members of your team when the entire project is completed. A peer evaluation form will be provided by your instructor.

14. Write a letter to a company in a <u>high-context</u> country to sell your new product.

15. Write a letter to a company in a <u>low-context</u> country to sell your new product.

TOPIC	**Using the Writing Process:** **Part 1 - Preparing to Write**
DEFINITION	Begin writing after you have planned what you are to do. The writing process consists of (1) planning; (2) composing, drafting and revising; (3) formatting; and (4) editing, proofing, and evaluating.
BACKGROUND	The fact is that people write in many different ways. You probably have your own plan for writing, and that is good. No matter what source you check out to see how to write, you will probably find that each source is basically the same.
	According to many studies over the past several years, employers are looking for employees who can write. In fact, one of the most valued skills by employers, according to recruiters, is for employees who can deliver a positive impression of the company through business writing. Memos, letters, and reports will represent the company to the outside world. If you want to climb the corporate ladder, you must learn how to write effectively.

KEY POINTS

1. **Planning**. Determine to whom the message is to be sent. What information will you need to give the reader?

2. **Composing, drafting, and revising**. After you have written down your plan, start composing what you are going to say. You will probably use one of the plans listed in this text as your guide. You probably will not get the letter ready for mailing until you have revised it several times.

3. **Formatting**. Keyboard the letter after you are entirely satisfied with what you have said and that you are certain the reader will know exactly what you mean.

4. **Editing and proofing**. Spend at least the same amount of time editing and proofing as you did on writing the letter—perhaps even more time editing and proofing. Find all errors. Make all corrections. Get someone else to proofread your work.

STEPS

1. Analyze your audience. To whom are you writing? You will structure your communication differently when writing to young people as opposed to writing to older people. What do you know about the receiver? What about the cultural background of the receiver?
2. Determine the purpose for writing.

103

      a. What do you want to accomplish and what can you do to achieve that purpose?
      b. Is your purpose realistic?
      c. Is your purpose timely?

3. Organize your thoughts.
      a. Prepare an outline of what you want to accomplish in the communication. Even before you prepare an outline, you may wish just to jot down some random ideas as these ideas appear to you.
      b. After you have written down a variety of random thoughts, organize those thoughts into a coherent plan. Some possible methods of organization are the following:

          1) Organize data by time. Arrange information chronologically.
          2) Organize data by classification: location, geography, division, section, product, service, or part.
          3) Organize data from most important to least important.
          4) Organize data from least important to most important.
          5) Organize data by categories, such as price, warranty, speed, print quality, and so forth.
          6) Organize data according to prescribed categories, such as personnel, budget, and so forth.

4. Write a first draft.
      a. Put your ideas into paragraph form. Be prepared to write several drafts before you come up with a final draft.
      b. Write concise paragraphs. Business writing should be brief. Comprehension rates decrease the longer the sentence (refer to the "rule of eights" for writing.)

5. Proofread and edit.
      a. Expect to spend about half of your time (or sometimes even more) on proofreading, editing, rewriting, and revising before your document becomes the final draft.

6. Check your work with the "C's" of business communication. A good check list you can remember is one where every word starts with a C. These C's should be applied in all of your business writing.

a. **Character/Consideration.** Use the YOU attitude in your writing. Make the reader feel as though you are talking directly to him or her. Use the reader's name in the communication whenever possible: (Thank you, Ms. Cummings, for the fine work you did on the project.) Respond to any communication you receive promptly—usually within three days, if possible. Use a positive tone rather than a negative one. Use "please" and "thank you" frequently. Use gender-fair and unbiased language. Treat everyone with equal respect.

b. **Conciseness/Concreteness.** Be specific, not vague. Avoid wordiness. Give essential information in as few words as possible. Avoid redundancies, idioms, clichés, euphemisms, slang, and jargon. Use short words; use short sentences and short paragraphs.

c. **Correctness/Completeness.** Use proper grammar and standard mechanics. Check spelling and punctuation. Proofread and edit. Then proofread and edit again. Reading the letter aloud can point out errors you never knew you had.

d. **Conversational Tone.** Use a friendly, helpful approach in business communications. Write as though you were speaking directly to someone. Picture the person or the person's business position in your mind as you write.

e. **Clarity.** Use vivid, understandable language. Your writing must not only be clear, but must be unmistakable. Two writing rules that will help you out are explained next.

7. **Rule of Primacy.** The **rule of primacy** is known as the rule of firsts. That which comes first gets the most emphasis. ("First impressions are lasting ones.") Place your most important idea to the *left* of the verb in the sentence. Example:

a. *Poor sentence:* **There will be a meeting today.** (The verb is "will be"; according to the rule of primacy, the word to the left of the verb is considered the most important word in the sentence—and "there" certainly is not the most important word in the sentence.) Unimportant words are called "expletives." Avoid expletives. Avoid expletives "it" and "there" when those words appear to the left of the verb.

b. *Better sentence:* **The meeting will be held today.** (The word to the left of the verb is "meeting," which is probably the most important word in the sentence.)

8. **Rule of Recency.** The **rule of recency** says that the information that appears near the end of the sentence is the *second most important* place of emphasis in a business communication. Example:

   a. **The meeting will be held today.** The **rule of primacy** says the most important word is the word "meeting"; but the **rule of recency** says the next most important word is "today," because "today" appears near the end of the sentence (actually, the word appears at the end of the sentence, which is even better.)

   b. **The board of directors hired a new CEO.** Rule of primacy: *important word(s)* - board of directors; *verb:* hired; rule of recency: *new CEO.* The "board of directors" gets the *most* emphasis in the sentence; the "new CEO" gets the *second-most* emphasis in the sentence. If you think the CEO is the most important item in the sentence, then rewrite the sentence to conform to the rule of primacy.

   c. **A new CEO was hired by the board of directors.** Now, you have given the "new CEO" the most prominence in the sentence and "board of directors" the second-most important spot in the sentence.

9. Define **demonstrative** pronouns (or words that *point out*.) Four demonstrative pronouns are used in business writing regularly: *this, that, these,* and *those.* For added clarity in your writing, **define** the demonstrative pronoun; in other words, **place a noun after a demonstrative pronoun** for even more clarity.

   a. Please give me those. (not clear)
   b. Please give me those *plans.* (clear)

   c. Those belong to Amy. (not clear)
   d. Those *ideas* belong to Amy. (clear)

   e. This is beautiful. (not clear)
   f. This *kitchen* is beautiful. (clear)

   g. These will never work. (not clear)
   h. These *processes* will never work. (clear)

10. Use proper sentence patterns for effective and clear communication.

   a. *Simple sentences.* Simple sentences contain **one independent clause**; that is, a subject and verb that can stand alone as a correct sentence and create a single idea. Simple sentences are used for **creating emphasis** and **getting the reader's attention**: (1) *The winter storm was scary.* (2) *Gerald was promoted to manager.* (3) *We must stop this silliness.*

b. *Compound sentences.* A compound sentence contains **two or more independent clauses** (sentences) joined by a comma and a conjunction (and, but, for, nor, or so, yet) or by a semicolon alone. Use a compound sentence to create a balanced relationship between the clauses that are joined. Your writing will then emphasize the idea that both clauses are somewhat equal in importance: (1) *We moved to Florida in 1999, **but** we stayed only five years.* (2) *Mary is an excellent manager; John is not an excellent manager.* (3) *The reports were late, **and** the entire team was fired.*

c. *Complex sentences.* A complex sentence contains at least **two clauses**: one independent and one or more subordinate clauses. A complex sentence is used to relate ideas to each other. Use a complex sentence in business writing to subordinate *bad news* to the reader. **The *bad news* is placed in the subordinate clause, and the good news follows in the independent clause:**

   (1) *Although James failed the final examination, he passed the course.*
   (2) *If you find that you cannot pay the entire amount at this time, please pay only the interest portion of the bill.*
   (3) *He knew that he was ill, but he recovered.*

d. *Compound-complex sentences.* A compound-complex sentence contains **three or more clauses**—at least two independent clauses and one subordinate clause. Use a compound-complex sentence to establish a series of complicated relationships among a series of ideas. Many times this type of sentence is used to "de-emphasize" bad news to the reader:

   (1) *When we lived in Alaska, we survived the cold weather; but we never felt that we were in danger from the cold.*
   (2) *Because I do not believe him, I feel for the safety of his children; the authorities have been notified to keep a close watch on the entire family.*
   (3) *If you ever get to Michigan, be sure to stop to see me; and we will spend a few days fishing in Lake Michigan.*

1. Search the Internet to find examples of redundancies, idioms, clichés, euphemisms, slang, and jargon. Find at least three examples of each. Compose sentences for each of the words. Submit the results to your instructor in memo format.

2. Write ten sentences that illustrate the correct use of demonstrative pronouns. Submit the sentences to your instructor in memo format.

3. Find a one-page article from a news magazine (*Time, Newsweek, U.S. News and World Report*, or others.) Make a copy of the article. Then search the article for violations of the rule of primacy and the rule of recency. Discuss your findings in groups of two or three.

4. Bring a business letter you may have received recently to class. Analyze the business letter for the many items talked about in this section. Discuss the letter with two or three others. Prepare a team memo and submit to your instructor.

5. Search the Internet or the library to find a list of common misspelled business words. Make a list of the words, correctly spelled. Use the list whenever you have some writing to do.

6. Study the punctuation, capitalization, and number writing rules Be prepared for short quizzes on punctuation, capitalization, and number writing rules.

7. You may want to practice some exercises on eliminating expletives and on defining demonstrative pronouns. Write several sentences that include expletives. Rewrite the sentences to omit the expletives.

8. What does the term *noun phrase* mean? Some additional terms that you need to know are the following: *independent clause, dependent clause, subordinate clause,* Use the Internet to find a definition and some examples of all these terms. Prepare a short memo to your instructor describing your findings.

9. Write five of each of the following sentences: *simple sentences, compound sentences, complex sentences,* and *compound-complex sentences.* Make the sentences business related. Attach the sentences to a short memo and submit the material to your instructor.

RESOURCES

www.junketstudies.com/rulesofw - discusses 11 rules of writing; includes tutorials.

www.grammar.ccc.commnet.edu/grammar - provides a thorough guide to grammar and writing.

www.mantex.co.uk - provides an opportunity to subscribe to a free newsletter on the rules for writing well.

www.writersblock.com - discusses writing software.

www.management.org/commskls/cmm.writ.htm - reviews writing topics relative to business communication.

www.klarti.com/business_writing - displays 10 steps for more effective business communication.

| TOPIC | **Using the Writing Process:**
Part 2 - Grammar and Additional Writing Guidelines |
|---|---|

DEFINITION The word "grammar" comes from a Greek word, *grammatikos,* which means "knowing one's language." Grammar is more than just a list of rules; grammar helps in understanding both the written word and oral speech.

BACKGROUND Grammar often refers to the correct or standard way to use the language. Business communication embodies a list of what is appropriate and what is not appropriate in the business world. Grammar makes clear the exact meaning of what is being said. Knowing the fundamentals of grammar is extremely helpful in business communication.

KEY POINTS

1. In order to improve your writing skills, you must have a solid foundation of grammar and punctuation rules.
   a. Effective business writing is concise writing that follows rules.
   b. Always use the "KISS" principle (Keep It Short and Simple) for the best business writing.

2. Remember the "**rule of eights**" for writing.
   a. The longer a sentence, the lower the rate of comprehension, according to the American Press Institute.
   b. Short, concise sentences consisting of **eight** words have the highest comprehension rate (100 percent); a sentence of 28 words in length has a comprehension rate of only 50 percent.
   c. The best length for a paragraph is less than **eight** lines.
   d. An effective paragraph discusses only one topic.
   e. For most writing, a paragraph is written in the direct pattern, with the main idea stated in the first sentence.

3. Use the following suggestions for writing effective paragraphs:
   a. Avoid abrupt changes in thought.
   b. Link each sentence to a preceding sentence. *(The butler enjoyed the bonus. The bonus was overdue.)*
   c. Strive for paragraphs that are consistently *deductive* (big idea first followed by details) or *inductive* (big idea before details.)
   d. Create emphasis in paragraphs by placing an important sentence either first *(rule of primacy)* or by placing the important sentence last *(rule of recency.)*

   e. Use *small* words and *short* sentences to make an

exciting paragraph:

NOT →*She will* endeavor *to be there on time.*

BUT → *She will* try *to be there on time*

    f.   Vary the length of the paragraphs—write short paragraphs and long paragraphs.

4. Compose exciting and effective sentences:

NOT → *There are* three people absent from work today.

BUT → Three people are absent from work today.

5. Write *positive* sentences rather than *negative* sentences—tell what *can* be done rather than what *cannot* be done.

NOT → Mr. Short will *not* call you until August 15.

BUT → Mr. Short *will* call you on August 15.

6. Use *active* voice to present *positive* ideas. The *subject* does the acting. "*Steve* wrote the report."

7. Use *passive* voice to present *negative* ideas. The subject is acted upon. "The *report* was ignored by Steve."

8. Use a word more than once in a sentence for *emphasis.* "The day was a *success,* and that *success* was due to you."

9. Use the following suggestions for adding emphasis:

    a.   Use lists to break up complex statements. Lists must be grammatically parallel in structure. Each item in a listing should begin with the same part of speech. You may number each item; you may give each item an alphabetical character; or you may use bullets or dashes for emphasis.

    b.   Use mechanical devices for emphasis. Many ways exist to add emphasis to your writing:

-special formats—lines or boxes used to set off material

-all CAPITAL letters

-*italics*

-a dash—within a sentence

-**bolding**

-<u>underlining</u>

-<u>**underlining and bolding**</u>

-color

ACTIVITIES

1. Complete an autobiographical research project online and to find out details of what was going on nationally, internationally, and locally the year you were born. You may wish to check the areas of sports, music, entertainment, politics, and TV. Be prepared to discuss your findings in class. Check with your instructor for length and format requirements for this assignment.

RESOURCES

www.chompchomp.com - online grammar resources; provides grammar explanations and interactive exercises.

www.grammarbook.com/ - provides grammar guides with answers to grammar and punctuation questions; free online quizzes for practice and review.

www.grammarlady.com - online reference for grammar and punctuation questions.

www.worddog.com - reviews documents and suggests changes for improvement; provides links to online dictionaries, encyclopedias, and quotations.

www.dictionary.com - gives links to Roget's Thesaurus and to hundreds of other online dictionaries, including non-English dictionaries.

	Preparing an Outline (example page 115)
TOPIC	
DEFINITION	An outline is a visual presentation of an assignment you are about to complete. Outlining helps you to organize your thoughts and gives you a chance to look at the overall picture before you begin the actual task. Writing from an outline results in a more logical and coherent final product. Your writing goes more smoothly and you save time as well.
STEPS	

1. Prepare a report; use the report title as the main title, center all caps at the top. Keep the heading specific.

2. Use upper-case roman numerals for the main headings of your outline (I, II, III, etc.)

3. Second-level headings may be numeric (1, 2, 3, etc.) or upper case alphabetic (A, B, C, etc.) depending on your style and word processing program.

4. Third-level subheadings may be lower case alphabetic (a, b, c, etc.), or numeric (depending on what type of second-level headings were used.) You want to alternate between alphabetic and numeric throughout the different levels of your outline.

5. The number of items under each heading or subheading will vary. You may not have to use a second or third subheading, but you should know how to organize a very detailed outline.

6. Avoid complete sentences; it saves time and helps you avoid long phrases in your outline, which defeats the purpose of an outline. You should focus on key words and phrases.

7. Stay parallel in the heading. Use all noun phrases or all participial phrases, all statements, or all questions.

8. Be consistent within each level of heading. If the first words are a noun phrase, then all of the first words should be noun phrases.

ACTIVITIES

1. Search the Internet for a variety of ways to prepare an outline. Present the results in memo format to your instructor and discuss your preference for preparing an outline.

2. Find out the meaning of "brainstorming." How does brainstorming help you in your writing? Pick a topic with a partner and see how many ideas each of you can come up with in 30 seconds or in one minute.

113

3. Using the Internet or the library, find a company yearly report. Study the report carefully; then prepare an outline of the report. Hand in the outline to your instructor.

4. Select an article two or more pages in length from a current magazine. Read the article carefully. Then prepare an outline of the article you have read. Hand in both the article and the outline to your instructor.

5. Check the Internet to find techniques other than brainstorming for developing ideas for writing. Make a list of these techniques, each with a short description. Submit the list to your instructor in a memo.

6. In one of the lecture classes you attend, prepare an outline of a lecture *after* you have listened to the lecture.

7. In the sample outline that follows, rewrite the outline so that each of the items is parallel within its category.

8. Choose an area of business you're interested in working in. Search the Internet for "jargon" in your area. Write a short memo to your instructor that includes ten items of jargon along with the actual meaning of the word or of the term.

RESOURCES

http://owl.english.purdue.edu/owl/resource/544/01/ - tips on how to prepare various types of outlines.

www.mindrelief.net/outline.html - information on outlining techniques and different types of outlines to use in your writing.

PLAN FOR NEW OFFICE CONFERENCE CALLS

Reginald Dennis

I. INTRODUCTION

   A. Background of problem
   B. Purpose of redefining costs
   C. Preliminary procedures

II. OBJECTIVES OF NEW PROCEDURES

   A. No setup fees
   B. No contracts or monthly fees
   C. Call anytime
      1. From anywhere
      2. To anywhere

III. BENEFITS

   A. Up to 150 participants at any one time
   B. International calls at 15 cents per minute
   C. Simplicity in set up and administration
   D. Operator help available 24/7
   E. Cost savings will show up almost immediately

IV. AVAILABILITY

   A. Begins May 1 this year
      1. Call extension 343
         a. Give your name to receptionist
         b. Ask for Form 45-B
      2. Alert your private secretary

TOPIC	**Preparing a Memo** (example page 117)

DEFINITION

A memorandum (memo) is an *internal* communication, whereas a business letter is an *external* communication. A memo is used to disseminate day-to-day information within the company and is considered less formal than a letter.

BACKGROUND

Memos may be written on a type of abbreviated company stationery. A memo may be preprinted with standard headings that can be arranged in a variety of ways and include: TO, FROM, DATE, and SUBJECT.

KEY POINTS

1. Type the headings using a proper memo format and fill in the appropriate information for each heading. Be sure to align the information as shown in the example memo on page 117.

2. Salutations and complimentary closes are not used in memos. "Sign" your memo by initialing at your typed name on the "FROM" line in your memo heading.

3. Use a triple space after the SUBJECT line and before your first paragraph.

4. Use block format. Single-space the material in the memo, but double space between the paragraphs.

5. Use the same organizational format that you use in letters; for instance, write the memo in *direct* style if the memo contains good news; write the memo in *indirect* style if the memo contains unfavorable news.

ACTIVITIES

1. Write a memo to all staff members congratulating each of them on the fine showing the company made in contributions to the United Way. Over $17,000 was collected from the 85 employees.

2. Write a memo to all staff members telling them that the day after Thanksgiving will be a workday. No one is to get the Friday off as a day of vacation.

Use all CAPS for headings
and align headings properly;
double space between

TO: Kay Johnson

FROM: Sally Smith *SS*

DATE: July 24, 20xx

SUBJECT: Conference Report

Single space
within
paragraphs;
double space
between

I recently attended the Academy of Business Administration Conference in San Antonio, Texas, to learn more about cultural diversity issues in the workplace. My overall impression of the conference was very positive. The following two topics were the focus of the session I attended on cultural diversity:

1. Legal ramifications and liabilities to the business should be of paramount concern to upper management. Personnel in management positions should be trained in all areas related to these issues via seminars provided by legal professionals.

2. Employee sensitivity to cultural issues in the workplace can provided for through cultural awareness training seminars. Each business should conduct assessments of cultural issues in the workplace to determine needs and issues to target in providing training.

I would be happy to share more information with you regarding the conference and what I feel would help our company to be successful in working with cultural diversity issues. Please contact me at your earliest convenience to schedule a meeting.

TO: All Employees

FROM: Jonathan Anderson *ja*
                  Director of Public Relations

DATE: April 20, 20xx

SUBJECT: Preparing a Memo of Transmittal

Please follow these guidelines in preparing reports or assignments for your supervisor. Always attach a memo of transmittal (internal communication) to the top of the report or assignment so that your supervisor will know exactly what the attachment is. *Note: If the report or assignment is to be sent outside the company (external communication), you may use a letter for the transmittal.*

The transmittal message gives you an opportunity to speak more personally to the primary read and reinforce goodwill. The message may include any comments that will stimulate interest in the report, confirm confidence in you as the writer, and perhaps lead to further interesting, responsible assignments.

Appropriate content for the transmittal message includes highlights of major findings, significant recommendations, comments about the research experience or the assignment, and an offer to discuss the report or assignment with the reader. You may also offer to assist with future projects.

TOPIC **Letter Style Formats** (examples pages 121-123)

DEFINITION Several different **letter styles** are used in business today. The most popular of these styles is the <u>full-block</u> letter style, where every line of the letter begins at the left margin.

Another letter style is the <u>modified-block</u> letter style, where every line begins at the left margin *except* the date line, the complimentary close, and the signature line, which begin at or near the center of the paper. In the modified-block letter style, paragraphs may or may not be indented.

Still another often-used letter style is the letter created by the Administrative Management Society (AMS). The AMS style letter does not have a salutation or a complimentary closing and is good for writing letters when the reader's name is not available.

Punctuation styles in letters generally fall into two categories. <u>Mixed punctuation</u> means that a colon appears after the salutation and a comma appears after the complimentary closing. Mixed punctuation continues to be one of the most popular styles of punctuation used in business offices. <u>Open punctuation</u> means **no colon** appears after the salutation and **no comma** appears after the complimentary closing.

KEY POINTS

1. Full-block letters may use either mixed punctuation or open punctuation. The examples in this unit will use mixed punctuation only. Remember-- every line in a full-block style letter begins at the left margin. Double spacing is used between paragraphs.

2. Modified-block style letters may use either mixed punctuation or open punctuation. The examples in this unit will use mixed punctuation only.

3. The AMS-style letter uses open punctuation. All lines begin at the left margin.

ACTIVITIES

1. Use the Internet to find an article about the importance of written business communication. Find information about the other letter formats like full-block style letter, the modified-block style letter, and the AMS-style letter. Discuss your findings with the class.

2. Collect various letter styles and bring to class for discussion.

3. The quality of the paper used for a company's letterhead is important. Use the Internet and find out all you can about letterheads and the quality of paper used for them. Prepare a short memo to your instructor with your findings. Cite the websites as the last item in your memo.

4. Find information on the Internet about addressing envelopes for business letters. Identify the guidelines for proper format used for business purposes. Be prepared to present your findings to the class.

RESOURCES

www.englishplus.com/grammar/letrcont.htm - provides a variety of letter-writing resources.

http://owl.english.purdue.edu/owl/resource/653/01/ - tips on writing the basic business letters.

www.libraryonline.com - resources for how to write a wide variety of business letters.

✦**Company Letterhead**✦

November 12, 20xx

Ms. Lorraine Beatty
Beatty Hair Styling Salon
987 West Harrison Street
Glendale, CA 98798

Dear Ms. Beatty:

This letter is an example of the full-block style with open punctuation. Please note that *all* lines in this letter begin at the left-hand margin. This style is a good one to use because you do not have to remember to indent paragraphs or other lines in the letter.

The material in each paragraph is single spaced, but you need to be sure to leave an extra space between paragraphs. This extra space is called *double spacing*. Note also that an extra blank line exists *before* and *after* the salutation (Dear Ms. Beatty). The only place you may vary the spacing of the letter is between the date and the inside address. If you have a short letter, leave enough space between the date and inside address that will cause the letter to look centered on the page. If you have a long letter, leave less space between the date and the inside address. Note that the person you are sending the letter to is part of what is known as the *inside address*.

The letter also illustrates *open* punctuation. Open punctuation means no colon appears after the salutation and no comma appears after the complimentary closing. Open punctuation is easy to use. *Reference initials* (the initials of the person who typed the letter) appear two spaces below the typed signature. An *enclosure notation* is placed below the reference initials when something is included with the letter.

I hope you appreciate the information in this letter and the attached rules of writing. Good luck in writing all of your letters. Be sure to proofread and edit carefully.

Sincerely yours,

Bob Hatchett

Bob Hatchett

Enclosure

✦Company Letterhead✦

November 11, 20xx

Mr. Jon Bigelow
987 North Sawyer Boulevard
Canton, OH 44238

> If necessary, you can reduce the number of spaces after the date line for longer letters so they fit on one page

Dear Mr. Bigelow:

This letter is an example of the modified-block style. Modified-block style means that the date line and the closing lines begin at the center point of the page. In the modified-block style letter, *you may* or *you may not* indent the paragraphs. The choice is yours.

This letter also illustrates the use of *mixed* punctuation. Mixed punctuation means that a colon is placed after the salutation (Dear Mr. Bigelow**:**) and that a comma is placed after the complimentary close (Sincerely**,**). In any style letter you write, you have a choice of using mixed or open punctuation. I chose to use mixed punctuation in this letter.

Some other facts about letters that may be helpful to you are the following. You may use bullets or numbers to highlight certain information.

- The name and address of the person to whom you are writing is the *inside address.*

- The greeting at the top of the letter (Dear Mr. Bigelow:) is the *salutation.*

- The body of the letter is made up of *paragraphs.* One blank line is included between the paragraphs.

- The *complimentary close* (Sincerely,) appears at the bottom of the letter above the writer's signature.

- The *signature line* is typed four returns down from the complimentary close. Write your name above the printed name.

This information should be helpful to you as you continue to write business letters.

Sincerely,

Ima Wright

Ima Wright

122

✦Company Letterhead✦

December 15, 20xx

The Michigan Letter Writing Corporation
12345 Lansing Street
Grand Rapids, MI 49501

SAMPLE OF AMS-STYLE LETTER

This letter is an example of the **Administrative Management Society (AMS)** style letter, sometimes called the **Simplified** style. This style is an efficient way of preparing letters and is especially good when you have a company name and address but do not know the reader's name.

Note that no salutation appears in the letter. The *subject* of the letter (SAMPLE OF AMS-STYLE LETTER) appears in ALL CAPITAL letters three spaces below the inside address. Then the first paragraph of the letter begins three spaces below the subject line.

Full-block style is used in the AMS-style letter. Since no salutation or complimentary close exists, you don't need to worry about open or mixed punctuation.

At the bottom of the letter, you will note that no complimentary closing appears. However, the typed signature with the writer's title is placed in ALL CAPITAL LETTERS five spaces down from the last line of the last paragraph Then the writer signs his or her name above the typed signature with title.

I hope you enjoy this little bit of information about the AMS-Style letter. You may have occasion to use the letter in the future.

Louise H. Wheelman

LOUISE H. WHEELMAN—OFFICE MANAGER

TOPIC	**Preparing a Letter or Memo in Direct Style**

Preparing a Letter or Memo in Direct Style
(examples pages 126-129)

DEFINITION

Direct style is used for "good news or favorable news" letters, such as letters of congratulations, order letters, request letters, favorable responses, routine inquires, and simple claim letters. Favorable news letters are relatively short—perhaps 75-100 words or less. The direct style may be used for memos as well as for letters.

BACKGROUND

Letters are typed on company stationery (letterhead), starting with the current date. Use the most common format for business letter-- a full-block letter style; that is, every line begins at the *left margin*. The full-block letter style is one of the most popular letter styles used in business.

STEPS

Three sections are included in a *direct style* letter:

1. **The objective.** The first section (usually one paragraph) should contain the good news for the reader: "Congratulations on your promotion." "Please send me the following items immediately." "Thank you for your kind words of sympathy." "The hard work you do for us is much appreciated."

2. **Facts, information, data, reasons.** The second section of the direct plan gives any information or factual material that will support the objective in Step 1. Use as many paragraphs as you need in order to give the reader all the information required. "Your 30 years at our company reflect well on you." "Your speaking of Sam so highly was comforting to me."

3. **Courteous closing.** Close courteously and politely. Perhaps add a forward-looking statement. "We look forward to working another 30 years with you." "Your kindness to Sam and to me will never be forgotten."

ACTIVITIES

1. Write a congratulatory letter (direct style) to a friend or relative who has achieved some special honor or award recently.

2. Find a scholarship awarded at your school or from another source. Write a letter in direct style applying for this scholarship. Be sure to address the criteria for this scholarship that you meet.

3. Send a direct memo to one of your co-workers expressing appreciation for a job well done.

4. You have decided to attend graduate school to work on an MBA degree. After studying the graduate catalog, you have narrowed your list of possibilities to three universities; but you are leaning toward attending Mid-State University in Ohio. Write a direct letter asking for all of the specific information you will need to know before you make your final decision. Some questions you want answered are the following:

   a. Approximately how much time is necessary to get the graduate degree? One year? Two years?
   b. Are graduate assistantships available? If so, how does one go about getting an assistantship?
   c. What are the grade-point-average requirements for getting a Master of Business Administration (MBA) degree?
   d. How many graduate credits can be transferred to the MBA program from another institution?

   You may have additional questions for which you need answers. Write the letter to the following person:

   Dr. Naomi Parks, Chair
   Department of Finance
   Mid-State University
   Pataskala, OH 43987

Regina Clause

604 E. Wisconsin Boulevard   Gaylord, MI 49431

September 1, 20xx

Mr. Robert T. Glockendorf, Sales Manager
The Independent Trailblazer Company
30987 West Georgia Boulevard
Cleveland, OH 43987

Dear Mr. Glockendorf:

Please send by UPS the following items from your fall catalog:

Description	Quantity	Price	Total Price
RJY Guitar	1	$475.59	$475.59
Guitar picks	5	30.00	150.00
G String	4	15.00	60.00
D String	5	15.00	75.00
Total			$760.59

My check for $760.59 is attached to this letter. I look forward to receiving the merchandise as soon as possible.

Very truly yours,

Regina Clause

Regina Clause

Enclosure

✦Company Letterhead✦

August 31, 20xx

Ms. Gretchen Long, Director
Library Services
Central Michigan University
Mt. Pleasant, MI 48859

Dear Ms. Long:

Would you please answer the following questions for me about how to list citations in a yearly report? Here are some of the questions I have:

a. How are Internet references cited in the footnotes of a report?
b. How are Internet references cited in the bibliography of a report?
c. Is it necessary to have a bibliography in a report if footnotes are used?
d. Are references from books, magazines, and other reports still cited in MLA format?
e. Do any businesses use the APA style of footnoting?

Your answers to these questions are desperately needed. Please call me at (989) 555-6666 at your earliest convenience.

Sincerely,

Rachael Wardrop

Rachel Wardrop, Director
Reports and Services

TO: Irene Clare, Assistant Manager
            Marketing Department

FROM: Rochelle S. Grafton, Manager *RSG*
            Marketing Department

DATE: August 1, 20xx

SUBJECT: Your Much-Deserved Promotion

Congratulations, Irene, on your promotion to Assistant Manager of the Marketing Department.

Your work for us within the department has been consistently outstanding over the nine years you have been with us. Your willingness to undertake any task or project is very much appreciated by all of us.

I look forward to working more closely with you and hope that you are with us for many more years.

✦Company Letterhead✦

October 1, 20xx

Mr. Ronnie Potts
1234 North Arizona Avenue
Sacramento, CA 98798

Dear Mr. Potts:

Yes, we will grant your claim for $45.98 you paid for a brand new garden hose that turned out to be full of holes.

We are sorry for the troubles you had with the hose, especially when it emptied too much water on your prize-winning pansies. Therefore, we are sending you a $500 gift certificate to replace the $195 worth of pansies destroyed.

We value your business, Mr. Potts, and hope that you will continue to purchase our products.

As a token of our appreciation for your business with us in the past, here is an additional coupon worth $50 off on your next order of garden flowers.

Sincerely,

Ima Dahl

Ima Dahl, Manager

Enclosures

| **TOPIC** | **Preparing a Letter or Memo in Indirect Style**
(examples pages 132-134) |
|---|---|

DEFINITION	*Indirect* writing style is used for giving "unfavorable or bad news"; such as, not getting a promotion, not getting a bonus, being fired by the company, or other negative messages. The goal of the writer is to keep the reader's goodwill and to get the reader to accept the unfavorable news.

EXPLANATION	Indirect letters or memos are typed on company stationery, beginning with the date. Use a full-block letter style; that is, every line begins at the *left margin.* The full-block letter style is one of the most popular letter styles used in business.

KEY POINTS

Four sections are included in an *indirect* style letter:

1. **The buffer** (1st paragraph). A buffer is a neutral opening that does not give a hint that the bad news is coming. Topics in this beginning section could be any of the following: compliment on past work; appreciation for company loyalty; agreement, facts, or understandings; thanks for past achievements.

2. **Reasons, explanation, facts** (2nd paragraph). The writer leads up to the bad news by cautiously listing the causes or the reasons for the unfavorable news before actually stating the bad news. Other topics the writer might cover are reader or other benefits, company policy explanation, facts of the situation, or evidence that the matter was considered fairly. Depending on the reasons and explanation, you may have one or more paragraphs in this section.

3. **Unfavorable news** (embedded in 2nd paragraph). Provide a clear statement of the unfavorable or bad news. Suggest an alterative, if applicable. Use embedded placement; *do not place the bad news as the first or as the last item in the sentence.* You may also *imply* a refusal rather than *state* the refusal outright. Perhaps you could come to a compromise with the reader. Be sure to include another sentence or two after the bad news so that the bad news is truly embedded.

4. **Close** (final paragraph). Give a forward-looking statement. Give information about an alternative you may have suggested. Offer your good wishes. Try to resell the reader on another idea if applicable. Close on a pleasant note.

1. You have received a letter from your landlord that notifies you of the date pest control services will be spraying your apartment. You are required to be at home during the time your apartment is being sprayed. You have a conflict with the date of the appointment and are required to notify your landlord in writing. Write an indirect letter to your landlord notifying him and providing an alternative to this situation.

2. Write an indirect memo to one of your employees telling that employee that he or she has not been at the company long enough to receive the annual Christmas bonus.

3. Respond to a letter from a person seeking a job with your company. Currently, you have no position available for a person in marketing research; nor do you anticipate that you will have an opening in the near future. No money is available for personnel. You know, however, that Seymour Company in your city is looking for someone in marketing research. You do appreciate the letter, and you are eager to help. Write the letter to the following person:

   Ms. Claudia Steiner
   30987 North Clare Avenue
   Mt. Pleasant, MI 48858

4. The local branch of the Independent Party wants to use your company auditorium for a rally they plan to hold in about six months. You do not want to get involved in any political activities. Write an indirect letter to the chair of the Independent Party in your city telling that person the reasons you cannot permit the party to hold a rally in your company auditorium.

✦Company Letterhead✦

April 12, 20xx

Ms. Irene Carr
Apartment 234
9874 West Main Street
Clare, MI 48853

| 1st paragraph - the buffer |
| 2nd paragraph - reasons and explanations given before bad news |

Dear Ms. Carr:

Your business with us over the past ten years has been very much appreciated. We always look forward to serving you in our store. Thank you for being such a loyal customer.

Our merchandise was available for inspection before you purchased it. Because the merchandise you ordered was sold "as-is" and without a refund policy, we cannot grant your request for replacement. Please understand our position and our policy.

In order to keep your goodwill, here is a coupon worth $25 on your next purchase from our store.

Thanks again for being such a loyal and caring customer over the years. We hope to continue to do business with you in the future.

Sincerely,

Richard Thomas

Richard Thomas
Accounts Receivable

Enclosure

MEMO .

TO: Harlan Parsons

FROM: Jessica Dowd, Director JD
             Human Resources Department

DATE: February 21, 20xx

SUBJECT: Your Request for Promotion

Thank you, Harlan, for the ten years you have been working with our company. You have been a loyal employee and have done your best with us.

Several people were considered for the promotion to director of your area. Two of the three people considered along with you have been here at least five years longer than you have. They, too, have been very loyal and dedicated to the company. Therefore, your request for promotion will be considered again next year; and, at that time, we see a great possibility that you will then receive the promotion.

Thank you again for applying for the promotion. We look forward to receiving your request next year at this time. Your dedication, loyalty, and creativity with this company, Harlan, are very much appreciated.

✦Company Letterhead✦

May 1, 20xx

Ms. Geraldine Pagemaker
987 North Calcutta Boulevard
Kent, OH 44240

Dear Ms. Pagemaker:

As a loyal customer of ours for the past 20 years, your business is very much appreciated. We have received your request for reimbursement of the latest order of plants you bought from us.

Because the asters were on a closeout sale and because we had marked the asters "as-is," we cannot refund your money simply because the asters died after only six weeks in the ground.

However, because we value your business, here is a coupon for $25 off on your next order of plants. Please be assured that we appreciate your loyalty, and we want to keep you as a customer for many years to come.

Sincerely,

Robert Moab

Robert Moab, President

Enclosure

TOPIC	**Preparing a Persuasive Sales Letter** (example page 138)

DEFINITION   Persuasive communications are used to sell products and services and to persuade someone to do something.

KEY POINTS

Four sections are used in preparing a persuasive sales letter using the A-I-D-A plan.

1. Persuasive communications use a definite plan to get the point across. Use the following four distinct sections:

A	→	Attention
I	→	Interest
D	→	Desire
A	→	Action

2. Several methods are used to attract ATTENTION in beginning the letter:
    a. Ask a question.
    b. Start the letter with a solution to a problem.
    c. Use a news announcement.
    d. Begin with a quote from a famous person.
    e. Use an analogy—compare something unknown with something known.
    f. Use an "If" opening or a "What if" opening.
    g. Use a pun or a play on words.
    h. Use the "You have been selected to. . ." approach.
    i. Begin with a short, funny story or anecdote.

3. After getting the reader's attention in a *short* paragraph, move on to the INTEREST section:
    a. Describe the product or service. Tell all you know about the product or service, such as size, color, shape, weight, etc.
    b. Describe what the product can do for the reader.
    c. Appeal to the emotions (love, goodness, joy); appeal to the rationality of the product or service (references to things like saving money, safety, or convenience.) Use human nature appeals such as to be well thought of or to be liked.)
    d. Use as many paragraphs as you need for this section.

4. Proceed to the DESIRE section. The writer's job is to get the reader to really *want* to buy the product or service. This section is written to reduce reader resistance and to convince the readers to purchase the product or service. Use as many paragraphs as you need.

a. Offer proof that what you are selling works.
b. Offer a guarantee.
c. Use a testimonial. What do others think about the product?
d. Use sincere language that people will believe.
e. Introduce price strategically (show the price in small units; compare the price with your competitors; show how the reader is saving money by purchasing the product; make your price a bargain; show how the reader benefits by taking advantage of the price.)

5. Stimulate ACTION. Get the reader to act. Use specific language to tell the reader what to do to get this product or service. One short paragraph is usually sufficient. Use one or more of the following suggestions:
   a. Make the action as easy as possible.
   b. Supply the reader with an 800 telephone number.
   c. Give the reader your website address.
   d. Offer an inducement or stimulus to get the reader to act quickly.
   e. Set a specific date to act (Act *now*! Order *by May 10.* Sign your name on the attached card *today*.)
   f. Use a postscript occasionally with another statement of action. A postscript stands out from the rest of the letter and tends to increase the chances for action from the reader.

ACTIVITIES

1. Prepare a persuasive communication for a product. Assume that you are preparing a sales letter that will go to over 100,000 people around the country. Study the product carefully; know to whom you are writing. Keep the letter to one page. Use the A-I-D-A approach.

2. Use the Internet to check information on writing a persuasive communication. Check to see what additional plans for gaining ATTENTION you can find. Check also to see what other ways to get ACTION exist. Use the information you have obtained to expand your ideas. Discuss your findings with other class members.

3. Use the A-I-D-A approach to prepare a one-page advertisement for the same product you used in Activity 1. Include computer graphics; prepare your ad on a standard sheet of 8 ½ by 11-inch sheet of paper. Print the ad in color, if possible. Use as many of the graphic capabilities as you need; *e.g.,* italics, bolding, underlining, different sizes of type, or a variety of type fonts.

4. Bring sample sales letters to class. Check your mail for examples of sales letters, or ask your friends and co-workers for samples they might give to you. Study the samples to see if they fit the A-I-D-A approach. Present your findings orally to the class.

5. Your sorority, fraternity, or club is interested in promoting a car wash this Saturday on the Commons at Central Michigan University. Cars will be washed for $5 each; the inside of the car will be cleaned for an additional $2. Write a persuasive sales letter to all the clubs and organizations on campus to encourage their members to take advantage of the car wash. Sign the letter with your name as Project Director.

RESOURCES

www.profitjump.com/articles - discusses persuasion as a convincing marketing tool.

www.marketingsource.com - provides shortcut ways to make letters more emotional.

www.writeexpress.com – provides resources, including templates, for your business writing needs.

PRO PRODUCTS, INC.

43 Main Avenue   989.555-9999   Ely, Ohio 43900

January 1, 20xx

Mr. Roberto Smith
12345 North Water Street
Kent, OH 44240

Dear Mr. Smith:

Are you tired of losing your pen? Do you ever run out of ink? If you answered yes to either of these questions, then read further!

With the new Giganto Pen you will never run out of ink no matter where you are. Losing your pen will be impossible with the Giganto Pen. The Giganto's ink cartridges last up to five times as long as the average pen. And, because of its size, the pen is easy to find when you're ready to write.

Your pen comes in 20 different colors and can write in black, blue, red, and green ink. Ten extra cartridges are included with the initial order of the Giganto Pen. The pen may be large in size but weighs less than one ounce.

How much would you pay for your Giganto Pen: $10, $20, $30 or more? If you act now, you can get your Giganto Pen, along with a total of 20 cartridges, for only $5.99, a bargain you cannot refuse. The pen is guaranteed to your satisfaction; and, if you are unhappy with your pen **at any time**, return the Giganto for a full refund.

To get your Giganto Pen, call toll free 1-800-GIG-ANTO or email us <u>now</u> at pen1@giganto.com. If you act within the next 24 hours, we will include a **second pen** at no additional cost.

Sincerely,

Roger Lodger Dodger

Roger Lodger Dodger
Sales Director

TOPIC	**Preparing a Persuasive Request** (example page 141)
DEFINITION	A persuasive request will call on the ability to persuade someone to do something that he or she may or may not want to do or to persuade him or her to your point of view.
BACKGROUND	Use the same A-I-D-A approach (explained in the previous section) used to persuade someone to buy something. This time, however, you are making a persuasive request that does not include selling a product or a service. You want something from the reader, so you must be very persuasive.

STEPS

1. **Gain Attention.** Start with a compliment or a fact. Ask an interesting question. Tell the reader the benefits to expect. You may wish to start by asking the reader for help.

2. **Build Interest.** Prove the worth of your request by providing facts, figures, and details. Show how you can be of benefit to the reader.

3. **Reduce Resistance (Convince, Create Desire).** Give counter arguments to possible obstacles. Know what you are talking about. Tell the receiver how he or she will benefit.

4. **Motivate Action.** Ask for specific action. Include an incentive. Set a date for action.

ACTIVITIES

1. As president of your collegiate marketing group, you have been asked by the executive committee to invite Dr. Rachael Collins, the national president of Marketers for Americans and a well-known textbook author, to speak to the annual conference of your marketing group, Marketers for Americans. Provide dates, times, possible topics, and any other information Doctor Collins will need to know. Anticipate what some of her objections or questions might be. Write to Dr. Collins at her home address:

   Dr. Rachael Collins, National President
   Marketers for Americans
   324 West Sycamore Avenue
   Grand Forks, ND 72401

2. Research spring break trips or some other vacation destination. Write a persuasive letter to your parents/guardian identifying the costs and the rationale for why you should be allowed to make this trip. Use a list in the body of your letter that identifies the expenses for this trip.

3. As president of the Marketers for Americans club at your school, you want to persuade the membership to take a field trip to an advertising agency in Chicago. You feel many benefits will be gained by all members. Write a persuasive memo to the Marketers for Americans that will convince them to use money from the group to sponsor the trip for all members.

4. Prepare a persuasive letter that can be used to convince local businesses to contribute prizes for your organization's fundraising event for a local charity. Items will be auctioned off at a dinner event next month.

5. Identify a situation in your own life that requires you to write a persuasive request letter. Prepare the letter for your instructor.

RESOURCES

www.instantsalesletters.com - provides information on creating sales letters guaranteed to sell.

www.salesletters.com - information and tips for using a sales letter to boost revenues.

www.marketingsource.com - provides many resources on marketing a business, including an article library.

www.ducttapemarketing.com/free-sales-letters - explains what makes an effective sales letter; how to write interesting and excellent sales letters.

398 West Main Street
Mt. Pleasant, MI 48858
November 23, 20xx

Senator Henry Goodfellow
40 Senate Office Building
3987 North Michigan Avenue
Lansing, MI 49348

Dear Senator Goodfellow:

How would you like a bright, efficient young woman to intern in your office this summer?

As a human resources major at Central Michigan University, I plan to receive a bachelor's degree a year from now. As an intern in your office, I would be able to handle correspondence from your constituents, run errands, answer the telephone and the email, and carry out other tasks that you ask me to do.

Although you haven't advertised for an intern, I have the feeling that if you find someone who will work efficiently, accurately, and intelligently, you would hire that person. I am that person, Senator Goodfellow.

After you have had time to study the enclosed up-to-date résumé, please call me any day between 9 a.m. and 5 p.m. at (989) 555-8888 to schedule a time that I can meet with you.

Sincerely,

Matilda Waters

Matilda Waters

Enclosure

TOPIC	**Goodwill Messages** (examples pages 144-147)
DEFINITION	Some communication in the business world is informal. Strengthening and building customer relations require a sincere, personal touch. At times, you will want to acknowledge the accomplishments of fellow employees and others in a friendly, informal way. When a message has no specific business objective, that message is called a *goodwill* message.
TYPES	**Thank you.** Send thank-you notes to someone who has done you a favor, or send a thank-you message to someone who has done a favor for the company.

Sympathy and Condolences. Notes of sympathy or condolence should be sent to an employee, customer, or supplier when any of them has experienced a loss, misfortune, or serious setback. Sympathy and condolences messages are often the most difficult messages to write, but they are often the most appreciated.

Appreciation. Send appreciation messages from a customer, a referral to a new customer, or an employee who willingly has worked overtime on a special project. All deserve to know how much they are appreciated.

Congratulations. If an employee or a friend receives a promotion, an award, is elected to an office on a board or organization, you should send a note to recognize the accomplishment. If you have personal relationships within the company, you may also want to send notes for weddings, a birth of a child, a graduation, or some other accomplishment. |
| **STEPS** | 1. **Goodwill messages should be prompt, direct, sincere, and concise.** Send your message as soon after the event as possible. Do not procrastinate. The *direct approach* is best, even with notes of sympathy or condolence. State the most important point of the message first; next, give a few more details, and finally, close in a warm, courteous manner. Sincerity and conciseness are part of all good communication.

2. **Do not give a sales pitch in a goodwill message.** Goodwill should be the *only* goal of the note or letter. |

3. **Avoid exaggerating your feelings.** "I can never express adequately my undying gratitude to you," is probably overstated. A simple warm, sincere thank you is much better.

4. **Keep goodwill messages to one page.** Goodwill memos and letters may be typed, although handwritten notes are appreciated. Sympathy notes should be *handwritten*.

ACTIVITIES

1. Write a letter of appreciation to Mr. Ralph Prescott, Director of Marketing, Prescott, Inc., 9878 West Michigan Avenue, Alma, MI 48856. Ralph referred two new clients to you, both of whom gave you large orders. Ralph's company was not able to accommodate the orders, so he recommended both of the customers to you. Tell Ralph how much you appreciate what he has done for you.

2. Ms. Ruth Stoddard, Director of Marketing and one of the employees you supervise, has decided to retire at the end of this coming year. Send Ruth a congratulatory memo praising her for her loyalty and service to your company for the past 25 years. Her work record is superb, and you are sad to think of trying to replace such an outstanding employee.

3. In two- or three-member teams, write a form thank-you letter to all of your national customers for their loyalty to your company. Assume any other information you wish to include in the thank-you letter. After the first draft is written, team members should proofread and revise the letter before the final copy is prepared. Present your letter to the class.

4. Send a sympathy note to Mrs. Lois Lansing, whose husband passed away after a lengthy stay in the hospital. Lois has been an employee of our company for the past 11 years. You may send the *handwritten* note to her through the company mail. Do not use email.

5. You will graduate from the university in a couple of months. Write a thank-you letter to your parents or guardians thanking them for all of the help and encouragement they provided you during the past four years. You feel that you could not have succeeded without their guidance and their great faith in your eventual success.

Jennings Products

43 North Highland Avenue   Phone: (989) 555-7777   Mt. Pleasant, MI 48858

April 22, 20xx

Ms. Lori Butler
Motivational Speaker
4987 Main Boulevard
Boca Raton, FL 33433

Dear Lori,

Thank you for speaking to our staff on "Motivation in the Workplace." You were a big success.

The employees of ABCD Corporation who heard your motivational talk last Wednesday thoroughly enjoyed it and learned a great deal about using motivation in the workplace.

As you realize, business employees have a social responsibility to become involved in issues and organizations within the community in which they live and work. Your talk enforced our thinking.

You are a wonderful example of the positive experiences that can result when interaction occurs. Thank you again, Lori.

Sincerely,

Robert

January 23, 20XX

Dear Carole,

Please accept our condolences on the recent death of your mother. We are all thinking of you and your loss.

Your mother was loved by all who knew her, and she was a real joy to be around. We will all miss her.

Please take as much time away from your job as you need. We look forward to having you back at your desk whenever you feel you are ready.

If any of us here at the company can be of help to you in any way, please let us know.

Reggie

Interoffice Memorandum

TO: John Turner, Maintenance Department

FROM: Clyde Littleton, Manager *CL*
            Human Resources

DATE: May 1, 20xx

SUBJECT: Our Appreciation

Your courage in stopping a fire before it could get a good start is beneficial to all of us. You were responsible for keeping the fire under control while the fire department was responding.

Had you not seen the smoke coming from behind the storage room door, the blaze would have been far out of control before the firefighters arrived.

Your keen observation and willingness to place your self in potential danger to help others is much appreciated by all of us. Thank you so much for what you have done for all of us, John.

TO: Holly Macfarlane

FROM: Audrey Williams, Human Resources *aw*

DATE: May 1, 20xx

SUBJECT: Congratulations!

Congratulations, Holly, on your recent promotion to Manager of the Human Resources Department at Clarkson Products. You are certainly deserving of that promotion.

We were sad to see you leave our company two years ago; but we knew at that time that you were moving to a position that would allow you to use your education and background to their fullest advantage.

Congratulations again, Holly. We miss you, and we wish you well in your new position.

TOPIC	**Intercultural and International Communication** (examples pages 156-159); (refer to Unit II, pages 97-99 also)
BACKGROUND	Appreciate the culture of other people instead of judging it. Avoid *ethnocentricity,* the feeling that one's culture is superior to all other cultures. Demonstrate sensitivity to both *high-context* cultures and *low-context* cultures.
DISCUSSION	In **high-context** countries, people do not feel comfortable committing themselves initially; they may seem intentionally vague. Examples of high-context countries are Japan, China, and other Asian countries.

Most of the high-context cultures rely on personal relationships to best establish the trust and background information necessary for continuing communication. Persons from high-context countries will seem to rely on *how* you express your message rather than on *what* you said.

Business and personal relationships are closely tied together. Expect decision-making to be collaborative and collective, and expect a reliance on trust or intuition. Be aware that contracts you make may change. Write or speak to high-context people using the *indirect* plan.

A person from a **low-context** culture may seem blunt or even rude in stating his or her position. Such communication is not considered rude in that country. Some low-context countries are Germany, Holland, Belgium, and the Scandinavian countries.

Many countries have aspects of both low- and high-context characteristics, such as the United States. People from these cultures will state what you think to be something obvious. Business and personal relationships are strictly separated in the low-context cultures. Persons in low-context countries are interested in explicit verbal communication to interpret what is meant. They are interested in what you actually say. Low-context people expect facts and statistical evidence. Write or speak to low-context people using the *direct* plan.

KEY POINTS

1. Use the *indirect* plan of communicating: (a) Begin with a pleasant opening; talk about the weather, your family, and other non-business issues; (b) Provide details, facts, and; (c) State the objective or purpose of your communication. Tell why you are writing or speaking; (d) Offer assistance. Close with a pleasant, forward-looking statement.

2. Use the *direct* plan in writing or speaking to people in low-context countries, such as Germany, Holland, Belgium, and the Scandinavian countries:

   a State the objective or the purpose at the very beginning of the communication.
   b Provide details, facts, and explanation.
   c Include a future-oriented final thought in a polite closing.

3. Follow these suggestions when writing or speaking to someone from another culture: (a) determine if the person is from a high-culture or a low-culture country; (b) use expressions that are easily understood by international people; (c) avoid controversial items; (d) use short, simple sentences; use short paragraphs; (e) include graphics and visuals if appropriate in order to get your ideas across; (f) use traditional format; you are not expected to know the letter styles of every country; the United States Post Office, however, will provide international letter-writing material if you are interested; (g) include a few words in the language of the country (salutations and closings are good) if you know any of those words; (h) avoid slang, idioms, jargon, redundancies, contractions, and clichés when communicating with people from other countries.

ACTIVITIES

1. Study the following nonverbal methods of greeting people in three countries. Then select five other countries and find the nonverbal methods of greeting for those countries using the Internet and the library. Present your findings to the class.

   Japan: a bow, as low as and as long as the other person's bow
   Greece: an embrace and a kiss on both cheeks or a handshake
   Australia: a warm handshake between men; shake hands with a woman only if she extends her hand

2. Search the Internet for information concerning international city and country telephone codes. Find the codes for at least ten countries and cities. (Example: The telephone code for Egypt

149

is 20; the telephone code for Cairo is 2.) Report your findings to the class.

3. Look for information about *gestures* used in other countries. Report your findings to the class. The following are three examples of gestures used in Germany:
    -Do not open a closed door without knocking.
    -Avoid the rude practice of chewing gum while talking.
    -Hold your thumb upright to signal the number one (1).

4. Use the Internet to find typical working hours in at least five countries. Discuss your findings with the class. Here are the business office hours of three countries:
    Brazil: 8:00 a.m. - noon; 2:00 p.m.- 6:00 p.m.
    Spain: 9:00 a.m.-1:30 p.m.; 5:00 p.m.- 8:00 p.m.
    China: 8:00 a.m. - noon; 1:00 p.m.- 5:00 p.m.

5. Jon has strong ideas about people in other cultures. Study the list and discuss each of the items after first coming up with a workable definition of culture:

    a   Culture is how everybody acts in their own country.
    b   Culture comes only from our parents.
    c   Location has nothing to do with culture.
    d   Everyone is just like me.
    e   I have everything going for me.
    f   Everybody speaks English; I do not need to learn a foreign language.
    g   They will respect my intelligence.
    h   We are all interested in getting things to go smoothly.
    i   They will see I mean what I say.
    j   Differences do not matter.
    k   I am certainly not ethnocentric.

6. If you were to visit Egypt, what would you like to bring home with you? Pick another country or two and answer the same question. Discuss with the class.

7. The Chinese and the Japanese use long periods of silence before answering a question. This practice is often confusing to many Americans and people from low-context countries. What is the reason for this practice? Contrast the differences in behavior between the people from the high-context countries and the people from the low-context countries.

8. Select a country in which you are interested. Research the country in terms of its cultural background. Compare the

differences with what the common practices are in the United States.

9. The following are some facts and information about Japan. Read and study the material very carefully. Prepare a memo to your instructor comparing these facts about Japan to facts in a low-context country. Read your memo to the class to generate a discussion.

-always punctual in business dealings
-entertainment after business hours is a part of doing business
-entertainment is NOT done in the home
-allow your host to pick the place for entertainment
-allow your host to pay the bill
-Japanese consider the word "no" impolite
-"yes" or "later" sometimes means "no"
-"I will consider it" probably means "no"
-giving and receiving gifts in Japan is a very common way of doing business
-do not call a Japanese person by his or first name
-use "san" following a Japanese person's last name (Sato-san; Motohiko-san), an honorable way to use Mr., Ms., and Mrs.
-do not give four (4) of anything in Japan; 4 is unlucky
-Japanese people understand what is left unsaid
-present your business card with both hands
-do not put the business card in your pocket; let it stay beside you on the table until your meeting is completed
-a smile can be used to hide displeasure
-pointing is impolite; blowing one's nose considered very impolite—especially at the table
-all gestures have meaning in Japan
-allow more personal space than we permit in the U.S.

10. As an international business person, research the Internet and the library for the time difference in selected countries. Knowing the exact time in a certain country is very important for phone calls and email. When the clock says 1:00 p.m. in the United States, be sure you know the time in Tokyo. Prepare material on time differences for class discussion.

11. Interview an international student on your campus. Ask the following questions: (a) How do the people of your country perceive Americans? (b) What are some of your positive and negative impressions of the United States? (c) What advice would you give to me if I were going to go to your country to live and work? (d) What are some communication barriers you encountered in this country? (e) What was the most difficult adjustment you had to make when you moved to this

culture? (f) What are some cultural differences? In addition, ask any other questions in which you have an interest. Prepare a memo that summarizes your interview.

12. Ask the person you interviewed for your international memo to come to class and talk with your classmates. They will no doubt have questions they would like to ask. Check with your instructor to see when a time for the speaker would be appropriate.

13. Place an "H" before the item that describes people from *high-context* cultures. Place an "L" before the item that describes people from *low-context* cultures. The answers are provided at the end of this section.

    a. _____ action-oriented
    b. _____ may seem blunt or rude
    c. _____ tries to save face
    d. _____ group gets credit, not the individual
    e. _____ uses *direct* approach to communication
    f. _____ does not enjoy saying "no"
    g. _____ uses *indirect* approach to communication
    h. _____ strong respect for rules and regulations
    i. _____ keeps business and pleasure separate
    j. _____ people seem to state the obvious

14. Underline the *idioms* (language peculiar to a people or a district, community, or class) in the following sentences. Then rewrite the sentences so they are clear and understandable to an international person. The answers are provided on page 155.

    a. We were caught flat footed.
    b. She is not feeling up to par.
    c. I need a ballpark figure from you today.
    d. Our five representatives really sent our sales into orbit last year.
    e. Hi Naoko. What's up?
    f. We will kick off the campaign on April 15.
    g. He put at least 12 grand into that project.
    h. Recent employment figures have us on the ropes.
    i. Stay with your newest employees until they see the light.
    j. He frequently shoots from the hip.

15. Prepare a list of high-context countries and a list of low-context countries. Prepare a memo for your instructor of your findings. Be prepared to present your findings orally to your classmates.

16. Write a letter to a Japanese businessman who plans to come to the

United States for a three-day business meeting at your company. In his letter to you, he requested two connecting rooms on the first floor of the hotel. He needs a hotel with a swimming pool because he is bringing his three teenage children (two boys and one girl) with him.

In addition, he requests that the meetings he is to attend be held each day in the morning only—perhaps eight o'clock until noon. He wants to spend the time with his children in the afternoons.

Although his children are not of baby-sitting age, he would like Someone to be with them in the mornings when he is attending the meeting. Perhaps this person could show the teenagers around town or attend nearby attractions. You are certain he wants his children to visit Central Michigan University as well as the parks, lakes, and picnic areas nearby.

You feel that you are able to grant all of his requests. You had originally planned to have the business meeting for four hours each day and the morning time is agreeable with you and your staff.

Write the letter to Motohiko-san in the *indirect style* at the following address:

> Sato Motohiko-san
> Toyohashi, Incorporated
> Go Toyohashi Macho
> Morikawa, Aichi Prefecture
> JAPAN 441

Study the examples of international letters before you plan and write the letter to Motohiko-san.

Here are some phrases that you may wish to use in writing to someone in Japan:

> Motohiko-san (a proper salutation)
> Sayonara (goodbye - can be used as a complimentary closing)
> Arigato (thank you)
> Domo arigato (thank you very much)

17. Letter – Direct Style. You have been invited to give a presentation in Munich, Germany, on how business communication in the United States differs from business communications in Germany.

Your audience will consist of employees from one of the larger companies in Munich, Autobahn Works Company.

You have a lot of information. You have studied all of the available travel guides (like Fodor manuals), books on how to act abroad, especially in Germany, and other sources. In addition, you have talked with several people who have lived in Germany for many years and two college students who spent a year abroad attending school in Munich. You feel that the information you have received is going to be helpful. You are to ask several questions about your presentation. How many people will be in attendance? How long should the presentation be? One hour? Two hours? Longer?

Your main objective in this letter is to have your reader reserve a room for you at a hotel that is near to the place where you will be speaking. You need a large room, one that has PC facilities, fax, and plenty of workspace, since you plan on doing a lot of work for your company while in Munich.

Write the letter in the *direct style* to the following person:

> Herr Karl Schroeder, Public Relations
> Autobahn Works Company
> Friedrichstrasse 498
> 87898 Munich
> GERMANY

Study the examples of international letters on page 15 and 159 before you plan and write the letter to Herr Schroeder.

Here are some phrases that you may wish to use in writing to someone in Germany:

> Very honorable Herr Schroeder (salutation)
> Auf Wiedersehen (goodbye)
> Danke (thank you)
> Bitte (please)
> Guten morgen (good morning)

RESOURCES

www.kwintessential.co.uk/resources/culture-tests.html - a great website to improve your intercultural communication skills; provides information and resources related to cultural awareness training and intercultural training; includes online quizzes to test your skills.

http://cyborlink.com/ – the web's leading resource for international business etiquette and manners.

www.culture-at-work.com/highlow.html - information on communicating across cultures with an emphasis on high and low context cultures.

Chaney, L. and J. Martin. In*ternational Business Communication, 2nd edition.* Upper Saddle River, NJ: Prentice Hall, 2000.

Neuliep, J. W. *Intercultural Communication: A Contextual Approach.* New York: Houghton Mifflin, 2000.

Reynolds, Sara and Deborah Valentine. *Guide to Cross-Cultural Communication.* Upper Saddle River, NJ: Prentice Hall, 2004.

Victor, David. *International Business Communication.* New York: HarperCollins, 2002.

Answers to Activity 13 (page 152) :

a.	L	f.	H
b.	L	g.	H
c.	H	h.	L
d.	H	i.	L
e.	L	j.	L

Answers to Activity 14 (page 152) :
-idioms underlined
a. We were caught <u>flat footed.</u>
b. She is not feeling <u>up to par.</u>
c. I need a <u>ballpark figure</u> from you today.
d. Our five representatives really <u>sent our sales into orbit.</u>
e. Hi Naoko. <u>What's up?</u>
f. We will <u>kick off the campaign</u> on April 15.
g. He put at least <u>12 grand</u> into that project.
h. Recent employment figures have us <u>on the ropes.</u>
i. Stay with your newest employees until they <u>see the light</u>.
j. He frequently <u>shoots from the hip.</u>

Suggested re-wording of sentences (answers can vary somewhat):
a. We were surprised.
b. She is not feeling well.
c. I need an estimate from you today.
d. Our five representatives really improved our sales.
e. Hi Naoko. What are you doing?
f. We will begin the campaign on April 15.
g. He put at least $12,000 into that project.
h. Recent employment figures have decreased substantially.
i. Stay with your newest employees until they are ready.
j. He frequently acts before he thinks.

ASUMI TRADING COMPANY, LTD.
Motohiko Sato, President and CEO
51 Morioka Machi
Moriyamaku, Nagoya 463 Japan

November 15, 20xx

Honorable Robert Goodman
Director of Sales
Mt. Pleasant Recreational Games, Inc.
123245 Main Avenue
Mt. Pleasant, MI 48858
U.S.A.

Allow us to open with reverence to you:

The spring season for cherry blossoms is here with us, and everybody is beginning to feel refreshed. We are all hoping that your family is well. We sincerely congratulate you on becoming more prosperous in your business. We hope that your winter is pleasant for you and for your family. You mentioned before that you like to ski. When will the weather in Michigan be available for skiing? Our skiing season began in late October.

We have an inquiry from a foreign customer and shall be very happy to have your best price and technical literature for the Michigan Surf Board. Here are the questions for your kind reply:

- What is the size of the surfboard? Length? Weight? Width?
- What colors are available?
- Are surfboards only for adults? Do you have surfboards for children?
- What safety features are provided?
- What additional information can you supply?

The above are all the questions I have for this inquiry. Please give us the information necessary about these surfboards.

We shall be very pleased if you will study the inquiry and let us have your reply as soon as possible. We solicit your favor. Please give our regards and greetings to your family.

Let us close with great respect to you,

Fumitashi Matsui

Fumitashi Matsui
Director of Sales

Berlin Motor Works

3498 Schroeder Strasse   **Berlin, Germany**

Herr Karl Weigland, Owner

November 14, 20xx

Fraulein Christina Boehmer
Recreation, Inc.
334 West Global Avenue
Normal, IL 61987
U.S.A.

Very respected Ms. Christina Boehmer:

Please send me information about four passenger paddleboats that are available from Recreation, Inc. Specifically, I need the following information immediately:

- What colors are available?
- What is the minimum and maximum speed of the boat?
- Can two people paddle or just one?
- What are the various models you have available?
- What are the prices of the various models?
- Does the boat have a back-up gear as well as a forward gear?
- What are the safety features?
- What additional information can you send me?

I will be pleased if you study my inquiry and write me immediately.

Danke,

BERLIN MOTOR WORKS

Karl Weigland

Herr Karl Weigland
Owner

SCHIEDA Manufacturing

30987 East Maintenance Way
Cleveland, Tennessee 35985

December 2, 20xx

Motohiko Oba-san, Director
Toyohashi Tatsuzawa Gakkan
4323 Fukiyama Macho
Kawasaki City, JAPAN 434

Oba-san:

Hello, how are you?   How is your weather now? The weather here in Tennessee is bright and sunny, but we are expecting some cool weather soon. At the end of August we had very heavy rains, and the streams and rivers were overflowing their banks. Today we are blessed with a very blue sky and a nice warm sun.

My company is sending me to Kawasaki City for a meeting with your company. I will leave here on December 10 and will arrive in Kawasaki City early on the 11th of December. I must leave Kawasaki City early morning on December 18.

I deeply request that you reserve a room for me at one of your hotels. I will need to be able to use my computer and my fax machine to do work for my company. I prefer a king-size bed; the room should be on the second or third floor.

I am hoping that you will be able to come for a visit to Tennessee this spring. We have a beautiful spring, and many flowers will be in bloom. Again, thank you so much for all you have done for me in the past. Best wishes to all of my friends in Kawasaki City and in Tokyo.

Sincerely,

Jonathan Russell
Jonathan Russell
Marketing Manager

MONTGOMERY INDUSTRIES

4987 North Industrial Park
Des Moines, IA 59878

April 15, 20xx

Herr Lukas Hoffmeister, Manager
Hoffmeister Iron Werks
3498 Burk Strasse
Bonn, GERMANY

Dear Herr Hoffmeister:

Please reserve a room with two double beds at the Bonn Palace Hotel for my visit to Bonn. My son will be accompanying me on the trip. I will need the room from April 30 through May 15. Please be sure the room has connections for the Internet. I will be using my computer throughout my stay to keep up with my business in the United States.

I will be free to meet with you daily, if you wish. I would prefer our meetings in the morning, but whatever time you have scheduled will be good with me. I would like a little free time to show my son some of the sights in Bonn and vicinity.

I look forward to seeing you on April 30. I will take a taxi to the hotel when I receive the confirmation from you.

Sincerely,

Georgia Montgomery

Georgia Montgomery, Vice President

TOPIC	**Email** (example page 164)
DEFINITION	Email is an electronic memo and allows almost instantaneous, text-based messaging over the Internet.
EXPLANATION	Email messages are prepared in a memo format with the standard memo headings already provided on your screen: TO, FROM, DATE, and SUBJECT.

1. Memos have always been reserved for internal communication within an organization only, but email has become widely accepted as a means of communication internally and externally.

2. Follow traditional memo format guidelines in creating an email message.
   a. Use block style and the direct pattern.
   b. Use paragraphs to organize your message.

KEY POINTS

1. Email has become one of the most preferred and most used channels of communication today.
   a. Email use saves time, money, and resources for businesses making email a valuable business tool.
   b. Business etiquette is different from informal; use correct capitalization, grammar, and punctuation. Avoid abbreviations and jargon.

2. A major concern when using email is "tone."
   a. Email is not considered the best communication method for creating relationships or for communicating emotions effectively.
   b. Email is most effective for sending the same message to many people, for communicating with individuals who are difficult to reach by phone, and as a convenient way to send an attachment.
   c. Email is most appropriate to use when you need to send a message that is not lengthy or complex and that does not involve confidential, sensitive, or emotional information.
   d. Do not use email to avoid direct contact when discussion is needed.
   e. Do not email a business contact or customer unless you have been invited to do so.
   f. Never use all caps in Internet communications; all caps is equivalent to shouting.

3. Email is business correspondence; always maintain a professional tone.

160

    a. Compose your message with the same care as
        when preparing any other written business document;
        proofread carefully and spell check your message.

    b. Always include a subject line that identifies the purpose of
        your message.

4. If a response is required, be sure to state the fact clearly in your
     message.

5. When asked to respond, do so immediately.

6. If information is requested that will delay your response, send a
     brief message to inform the sender.

7. Be sure to refer to an attachment specifically within the
     message itself.

8. Do not forward a message without permission.

9. Do not send personal emails on company time.

10. Email may not be the best way to communicate if you need
      an immediate response from people for a number of reasons:
        a. They do not use email or do not like to use email.
        b. They may not check their email regularly.
        c. They may be overwhelmed with email messages and
           yours is just one more.

11. Email provides a real threat to corporate security as email
      usage continues to increase. **Caution:** Do not send
      confidential or highly sensitive information through email; use
      the telephone or face-to-face meetings instead.

12. As with any written communication, email is a permanent
      document and can easily be saved and printed. Most
      importantly, an email message can easily be forwarded to
      anyone in a matter of seconds. **Caution:** Do not put anything
      in an email message you would not want anyone else to see!

13. Liability issues, combined with employee abuse of email and
      Internet usage, has resulted in the need to monitor employee
      usage. Be sure you follow the "acceptable usage policy" for
      your company regarding Internet usage to avoid losing your
      job!

        a. Many organizations have implemented Internet usage
           policies to cover all aspects of company email; such as,
           acceptable use, sending abusive email messages, email

retention, company's right to monitor, access and security issues, software and system usage, personal use, appropriate Internet usage, copying or downloading copyrighted materials, no expectation of privacy on company network, and more.

    b. Many organizations monitor employee usage of email and the Internet as a means to enforce their Internet usage policy and to reduce their liabilities.

ACTIVITIES

1. In small groups, brainstorm to identify at least five advantages and five disadvantages of using email.

2. Conduct a class debate concerning Internet usage policies.
   a. Form teams for each side of the debate (organization vs. employees.) To prepare, do some research to find examples of company Internet usage policies or check with local employers to find examples.
   b. Find news articles about current instances or lawsuits dealing with this issue.
   c. Consider what the pros and cons are for each side. What are the reasons for an organization to monitor employees and/or implement an Internet usage policy?
   d. What are the ethics and rights of the organization to the individual involved? Would you work for a company that did not allow you to send or receive personal email at work?

3. For each of the situations listed below, discuss whether email would be the best communication channel to use and why:
   a. A new account representative needs to introduce herself to her 25 clients.
   b. Request information from a colleague who works in the overseas office.
   c. The time for a meeting has changed from tomorrow at 9:30 a.m. to 1:30 p.m.
   d. Send a list of customers and account numbers to a colleague in a branch office.
   e. Send the corporate phone directory to a new employee at his home office.
   f. After a disagreement in a meeting with a colleague, you want to communicate your regrets for any hard feelings.

4. Find a copy of a company's "acceptable usage policy". You can find one or more policies on the Internet, you can ask someone for a copy of their company's policy, or you can bring in a copy from your own employer. Find news articles about recent cases involving the termination of employment based on

a breach of such policies by employees. Discuss the key issues that resulted in these terminations and look for similarities between these terminations.

RESOURCES

http://office.microsoft.com/en-us/outlook-help/12-tips-for-better-e-mail-etiquette-HA001205410.aspx – Tips for improving your email etiquette.

www.101emailetiquettetips.com/ - 101 email etiquette tips and resources related to email etiquette.

Email program provides memo headings automatically, including date; don't include these headings again in your message

From: Jasmine Thompson
Sent: Wed 8/11/20xx 2:33 PM
To: Todd Smith
Cc:
Subject: Program revisions

Include salutation when message is sent outside the company

Dear Todd:

We have just completed the program revisions you requested. We were able to keep the information you prepared in the format you desired for the primary document and still stay within the page number limitations. The final documentation will be sent to you when we receive your reply to this message.

We hope you are satisfied with the work we have completed and look forward to doing business with you again in the near future. It has been our pleasure to serve you.

Sincerely,

Jasmine Thompson

Use a complimentary closing and include your name when a salutation is used

Always request a reply if required and deadline if appropriate

164

| TOPIC | **Netiquette** |

| DEFINITION | Use of proper and acceptable practices when communicating on the Internet, including using email and especially for business-related purposes, is called "netiquette." |

| EXPLANATION | Knowing and following proper netiquette is important. Conventions for acceptable usage and formatting guidelines continue to develop for the use of email, discussion lists, blogs, Twitter, and other forms of Internet communication. |

KEY POINTS

1. Internet communication such as email and discussion boards are typically instantaneous. Don't forget to consider how your remarks may or may not be interpreted by others. When sound and body language is absent, text alone can be misconstrued. Humor is often lost in the transmission and can be easily misinterpreted.

2. If in a discussion list, stick to the subject. Look at what others have already said before you post to avoid repeating something just discussed. Review archives as well.

3. Do not make statements that could be interpreted as an official representation of your employer or as offers to do business.

4. Never be rude or inflame someone (known as "flaming".) Flame wars can create serious problems such as receiving unwanted mail and cluttering mailboxes.

5. Don't type anything you wouldn't tell someone "face-to-face." Someone can easily forward your communication to others, print it, or show it to others without your consent.

6. Do not send or forward junk email, including jokes, chain letters, and other types of spam.

7. As explained previously, don't use all caps (the equivalent of cyber shouting), always fill in the subject line, and be sure your reply refers to the subject.

8. Avoid password security problems. When a website asks if you want them to "remember" your password for future visits, say "NO!"

1. Prepare a memo to all employees about the importance of netiquette in the workplace. Include the at least three specific netiquette issues your company wants all employees to be informed of. Refer employees to at least one Internet website you feel will provide them with further information on netiquette.

2. Find a copy of a company's acceptable usage policy and see what points in their policy may or may not relate to netiquette. Discuss improvements or potential loop holes that may exist in the company's policy as it relates to netiquette.

RESOURCES

www.dtcc.edu/cs/rfc1855.html - guidelines for netiquette which organizations may use in creating their own policy.

www.netmanners.com/email-etiquette/category/email-etiquette-articles/ - library of articles related to all aspects of email and netiquette including the dos and don'ts.

TOPIC	**Cell Phone Etiquette**
EXPLANATION	The lack of respect for others due to the improper use of cell phones in public has led to the need for cell phone etiquette. Rules for the courteous use of cell phones are being developed and publicized to promote good manners for cell phone usage and to avoid over exposure to "second-hand conversations."

Knowing and following proper cell phone etiquette is important. Conventions for proper use of cell phones continue to develop. Every business person who relies on their cell phone needs to know and practice cell phone etiquette.

KEY POINTS

1. Respect the rules when asked or as posted in an establishment regarding usage of cell phones including texting. Turning your cell phone on vibrate is not acceptable in situations where cell phones can interfere with other equipment such as on airplanes and in hospitals.

2. Don't infringe on others' personal space, both physical proximity and sound. Be mindful of how close you are to others when using your cell phone in a public place and lower your voice. You may not think you're talking loudly on your phone; but if everyone around you can hear you, you're invading their personal space.

3. Don't talk or text on your cell phone when in the company of others. If you must take the call, tell the caller you will call him or her back and end the call immediately. Be sure to apologize for the interruption. When necessary to take a call, excuse yourself from the presence of others and make the conversation brief. Carrying on a cell phone conversation while others have to listen and wait for you to finish is rude and unprofessional.

4. When alone in a restaurant, follow the lead of others. If no one is using a cell phone, then the use of the cell phone is likely to be frowned upon. Some restaurants cater to business people, and the use of cell phones by diners is much more acceptable. Whatever the situation, remember not to infringe on the personal space of others.

5. Some situations occur where you simply should not bring your cell phone: funerals, weddings, church services, and a job interview are a few examples. Another good rule for proper cell phone usage is if the lights are off, your phone should be off.

7. Do not set your cell phone to an annoying, elaborate ring tones or a melody that rings continuously until answered. These elaborate "rings" are perceived as unprofessional; the noise pollution is unnecessary. What might be a cute ring tone around your friends is not going to impress your boss or clients.

8. Don't let text messaging damage your writing skills! The extensive use of text-based abbreviated communications today is showing up in the more formal writing of young people today. These shortcuts should never be used in professional and business writing, including emails. Always be professional in your formal writing… remember that the personal pronoun "I" must be capitalized and proper grammar and punctuation is a necessity. Check out this article about the effects of texting on writing: www.timesdaily.com/article/20090716/ARTICLES/907165030?Title=Does-texting-hurt-writing-skills-.

ACTIVITIES

1. As a class or in groups, make a list of bad cell phone manners you have witnessed or committed yourself. Once your list is completed, discuss each "infraction" and identify what should have been done. Are there instances where cell phone etiquette is different for personal versus business situations?

2. See if your cell phone manners are up to speed. Take the cell phone etiquette quiz at the following website: www.letstalk.com/company/release_031406.htm

RESOURCES

www.letstalk.com/promo/unclecell/unclecell2.htm - provides an etiquette guide for the proper use of cell phones.

www.microsoft.com/smallbusiness/resources/technology/communications/cellphone.etiquette - shares a 10-point plan for using proper cell phone etiquette.

TOPIC **Preparing Reports** (examples pages 173-174)

TYPES Terminology for the different kinds of reports varies, but reports can be divided into three major types: those that inform, recommend, or instruct.

In this unit you'll learn how to prepare informational reports and analytical reports.

Informational reports are those reports that provide information only. Usually no analysis of the data is given. Informational reports simply present information in an objective, organized way. The report writer(s) will need to gather and present the information in the appropriate report format. The memo format is used for internal reports (unless more formality is called for.)

Analytical reports involve research, interpretation, and recommendations. Writing this type of report requires critical thinking to analyze the problem and the research in order to make recommendations.

BACKGROUND Information provided in a report will help busy executives or employees make a more informed decision on a particular project or area of study. When a business (or your boss) needs information in a nice, neat package a report is often just what is needed. The person or persons who are charged with writing the report are often selected because they possess the needed information and/or the expertise in that area. Most companies are trying to curtail the length of reports because most people just do not have the time necessary to read a long report. Once in a while, however, you may need to prepare a long report due to the subject matter of the report.

KEY POINTS

1. Think of a report as having three major components.
   a. Front-end materials
   b. Report body
   c. Back-end materials

   A more formal and lengthy report may have many more "front-end materials" such as a cover page, table of contents, and executive summary. The report body itself will consist of an opening, body, and the closing. The "back-end materials" can include appendices and bibliography as needed

2. Planning is key and saves time in the long run. Know your target audience and the scope of your report.

3. Prepare by creating an outline. You'll need to identify the major sections of your report. Creating an outline will help organize the logic and flow of your report BEFORE you begin writing. Organizing what you want to include in an outline will help you put your report in perspective.

4. Do your research. Gather your information and/or the data you'll need in order to write the report.

5. Organize the report into the appropriate report format. Some companies have a company manual that gives an accepted format for preparing reports. Generally, the formality of your report and your target audience will dictate the appropriate format. Note: memo format is used only within a company.

6. The writing process begins once your outline is complete with the all the facts and information you need. Use the major sections of your outline as informative headings in your report. Informative headings (not generic headings) will give your report high skim value and be reader friendly. Refer to the informational report template on page 172 also.

7. Write the introduction. The introduction will orient your readers to your report if you explain the what, why, and how. The introduction to a report contains some or all of the following parts:

   a. Authorization and Background. Usually at the beginning of the report you will have a short section that gives a little background about the report; namely, who authorized the report, why the report was completed, and who was involved in completing the report.

   b. The Problem Statement. What is the topic of the report? What are you writing about? The statement of the problem should be direct and to the point.

   c. Purpose of the Report. Why did you prepare this report?

   d. Scope and Analysis. What is covered in the report? What is not covered in the report?

   e. Delimitations. What controls have you, the writer, placed on the subject? A report cannot cover every detail of every explanation. What have you decided to include in the report?

170

   f. <u>Limitations</u>. What factors do you not have control of in this study? What factors are inherent in the study itself?

8. <u>Report Body</u>. Report on the major points. Include informative headings and avoid lengthy paragraphs. See the informational report template on page 172.

9. <u>Front-end Materials</u>. After the report has been completed, you may wish to add a title page. A memo of transmittal may also be included. This memo transmits the report to the person or persons for whom you prepared the report. Business people have many projects being carried out simultaneously. A memo of transmittal will recall the original project for the reader. If the report is lengthy (over three pages), you made need a table of contents and/or an executive summary of the report so that the gist of the report can be understood quickly.

10. <u>Back-end Materials</u>. As necessary, you should include a bibliography and appendices in the back-end materials of your report.

RESOURCES

http://owl.english.purdue.edu/owl/resource/726/01/ - great resource for all types of writing; this link takes you to their handbook on report formats.

http://www.census.gov/ - a great source for statistics related to the United States.

http://owl.english.purdue.edu/owl/resource/560/01/ - this link takes you to all the APA guidelines with great examples and easy-to-follow directions.

www.apastyle.org/ - website for the American Psychological Association, publisher of APA style products.

www.wordbiz.com/archive/7tips_effective_reports_Suze_St_Maur .shtml - easy-to-read article providing 7 tips for writing effective reports.

www.surrey.ac.uk/Skills/pack/report.html - discusses effective report writing in higher education and the workplace.

www.impactfactory.com/p/report_writing_skills_training/friends_ 1·151-2105-94958.html - provides "14 simple steps" to effective business report writing.

Informational Report Body Template – Memo Format

TO: Reader of the report

FROM: Your name

DATE: Current date

SUBJECT: Report topic

> Triple space before the first paragraph and before headings (these are Level APA headings)

Begin with an introductory paragraph—a short section that may include some or all of the parts explained on pages 170-171 (authorization and background, the problem statement, the purpose, scope and analysis, delimitations and limitations.) You should also introduce the main points that you'll be discussing in the body of your report in the form of a list, if appropriate, like this:

1. Main point 1
2. Main point 2
3. Main point 3 (etc.)

The Middle of Your Report – Covering Your Main Points

The middle of your report should be divided into sections to report on each of the major points to be discussed. Include an informative heading for each main point to improve readability. You may need multiple paragraphs for each main point. Follow APA style guidelines for formatting headings and the appropriate level of headings to use (Level 1, Level 2, Level 3, etc.) Refer to the APA style guidelines for headings at http://owl.english.purdue.edu/owl/resource/560/16/.

The Closing of Your Report

The purpose of an informational report is to provide information. To conclude your report you can review the main points, provide supplementary information, offer to follow-up with additional information, and/or provide suggestions for what should be done next. If the situation warrants, you should thank others for their assistance or support as well.

TO: Jan Banning

FROM: Lyn Wong *LW*

DATE: July 20, 20xx

SUBJECT: Report on Academy of Business Conference

I recently attended the Academy of Business Conference in San Antonio, Texas, to learn more about cultural diversity issues in the workplace. My overall impression of the conference was very positive. Two topics were the focus of the session I attended on cultural diversity: (1) legal ramifications and (2) employee sensitivity.

Legal Ramifications

Legal ramifications and liabilities to the business should be of paramount concern to upper management. Personnel in management positions should be trained in all areas related to these issues via seminars provided by legal professionals.

Employee Sensitivity

Employee sensitivity to cultural issues in the workplace can provided for through cultural awareness training seminars. Each business should conduct assessments of cultural issues in the workplace to determine needs and issues to target in providing training.

Implementation and Follow-up

I would be happy to share more information with you regarding the conference and what I feel would help our company to be successful in dealing with cultural diversity issues. I was able to gather valuable materials to share with our staff members. I am looking forward to planning a cultural awareness training session focusing on legal ramifications and employee sensitivity for all employees before year end. Please contact me at your earliest convenience to discuss these plans and schedule a meeting. Thank you for the opportunity to attend this conference.

TO: Jerrod Basha

FROM: Mary Tofston*MT*

DATE: September 18, 20xx

SUBJECT: Survey Results on the Fab 2000

We have completed our survey on our new vacuum cleaner, the Fab 2000. The following section reports our findings and analyses of the survey results related to consumer response to the Fab 2000 Model.

Recommendations for Improving Sales

To improve the potential sales of the Fab 2000, we recommend the following changes be made prior to market release:

- Prepare a more detailed owner's manual that includes pictures of each component.

- Reduce the retail price to better compete with the Hoover XLR model.

Fab 2000 Survey Findings and Analyses

The preliminary assessment of the survey data found the Fab 2000 well received by consumers. Over 75 percent of respondents found the new features of this model appear to make the model very attractive to consumers over the nearest competition.

The overall design of the Fab 2000 was also appealing to 68 percent of the consumers surveyed. However, a common concern was whether the cord would hold up with heavy use.

The majority of consumers (62 percent) responded favorably to all categories on the survey concerning convenience, ease of use, design, and suction power.

TOPIC	**Justification Report** (example page 177)
DEFINITION	A justification report describes and provides reasons for an action. A justification report describes an exception to a policy or a practice and attempts to justify that exception. A justification report uses an appropriate personal, courteous, and confident tone.
BACKGROUND	The justification report is another informal type of report. Usually, a justification report is no longer than a page or two and may take the form of a memo (internal report) that circulates within an organization or in letter format (external report) that is sent outside the company.

KEY POINTS

1. **Introduction.** Identify the problem that exists and clearly explain the problem. Give a detailed background of the problem.

2. **Recommendation.** Propose a solution or make a recommendation.

3. **Implementation.** Explain how and when the recommendation should be put into effect.

4. **Conclusions.** Briefly states the advantages of adopting the recommendation or recommendations.

5. **Justification of Conclusions.** Explain why the conclusion is appropriate.

STEPS

1. Use memo format to prepare the justification if the report is to stay within the company.

2. Use letter format to prepare the justification if the report is to go outside the company.

3. Keep the justification short. Rarely will you have a report more than two or three pages. Give appropriate emphasis to each of the headings.

1. Study the sample of a justification report on the following pages. Discuss the report in groups of three. Be prepared to present the highlights of your discussion to the class.

2. Survey the library and the Internet to find examples of justification reports. Report your findings to your classmates.

3. Prepare a justification report based on the following incident: In order to reduce expenses, the Marketing Department of your company plans to layoff 15 of the most recently hired employees. The company has experienced a dramatic drop in sales over the last six months, creating a cash flow problem.

   Send the memo to all employees from you, the Director of Marketing. The memo must be sensitive to the feelings of those being laid off. Do not promise the employees anything you cannot carry out. Those employees to be laid off will be the last 15 hired by the company. Some of them have been with the company over two years—one or two of them even longer.

   Be sensitive to the feelings of those being laid off. You can strongly suggest that if things improve within the company during the next six months, a good chance exists that they will be hired back—but, again, you cannot promise them they will definitely get their jobs back.

   Most of the 15 employees showed a lot of promise and would have undoubtedly moved up within the company.

Interoffice Memorandum

TO: Ms. MaryAnn Lucas, CEO

FROM: Your Name, Human Resources Manager

DATE: Current Date

SUBJECT: Justification of Override of Company Policy

Introduction

Richard Tilden, Sales Representative, filed a request that he be paid his commission on the sale of a laptop computer. Mr. Tilden was originally denied his commission because he did not check with his supervisor before he gave a customer a discount on the computer even though the computer was a different model from the one that was supposed to be discounted.

Recommendation

The recommendation for Richard Tilden is that he be paid the full commission on contract No. 34987, even though he gave the customer a special discount on a model that was not to be discounted at this time. The recommendation is that he should not be required to cover the price differential out of his own pocket.

Justification

This exception for Mr. Tilden is justified for five reasons:

1. Mr. Tilden made the contract adjustment in good faith, attempting to salvage the account.

2. The sales closing procedure has been reviewed with Mr. Tilden, and he has demonstrated the procedure to a group of trainees and a group of interns. I am convinced he will not repeat the error nor make price discounts unnecessarily in the future.

177

3. Mr. Tilden has experienced excessive medical expenses related to his wife's chronic illness. The commission is significant to him, but relatively insignificant to the company.

4. This action is an opportunity to demonstrate our faith in Mr. Tilden and build the morale and the motivation of a potentially excellent to outstanding sales representative.

Implementation

The commission that Mr. Tilden earned will be added to his next paycheck, according to company policy.

Conclusion

The decision should affect Mr. Tilden in a positive way. I feel that he will be more productive in his commission dealings in the future. I feel, too, that he will be very careful to apply company policy to all situations in the future.

Justification of Conclusions

Mr. Tilden's work for the company has always ranged above average to excellent. By paying him the full commission, his work will no doubt continue to be positive. He is a valuable employee; we do not want to lose him.

TOPIC	**Accident Report** (example page 181)
DEFINITION	An accident report, sometimes called a trouble report, relates in detail that an accident has taken place in the company and on company time.
STEPS	1. **Introduction and Background.** Give a brief background that includes the fact that an accident happened. Include the date, the time, the place, and the people involved. Also list all of the people and titles who become involved by virtue of the accident (*e.g.*, the union representative and any others.)
	2. **Accident Summary.** As the one who will write the final report, summarize all details of the accident. Be sure your notes are thorough enough to help you prepare your report. Interview the participants, if necessary, so that you have all the facts.
	3. **Chronological Details.** Enumerate the findings and complete details of the accident in the order of occurrence. Be sure each detail is complete and that your report tells clearly what happened.
	4. **Corrective Actions.** Tell what needs to be done to prevent such occurrences from happening in the future
ACTIVITIES	1. Search the Internet to find out information about accident or trouble reports. Prepare a list of sources that you submit to your instructor in memo format.
	2. Prepare an accident report from the information that follows. Use memo format and submit the report to the company CEO, Alice Parsons.

Details of the Accident

Assume when you came to work May 1, 20xx, which was on a Thursday, one of the employees, Justin Peck, walked into the conference room at the beginning of the work day. Justin did not realize the overhead projector had been moved to a different location in the conference room by the secretary, Meg Anderson. Justin was going to the conference room to practice for a presentation he was to give later in the day.

The cord from the projector was on the floor just inside the door to the conference room. Justin entered the room, tripped on the cord, and fell to the ground. In an attempt to break his fall, he reached for the table in the room to steady his fall; but his arm did not reach the table. Justin fell to the floor, hitting his left arm against the table. The arm was broken in two places. In addition, Justin had a large cut on his cheek caused when he scraped his face on the table as he fell.

The secretary, Meg Anderson, hearing the noise and the shouts, ran into the conference room. She saw Justin on the floor and immediately called 911 before bending over Justin to see how badly he was hurt. In addition, Meg called to another secretary, Claude Russell, to help get Justin into a chair. Claude thought they should not move Justin until the EMT team arrived. Meg agreed. So they covered Justin with a blanket from the closet to keep him warm and perhaps prevent him from going into shock.

The EMT team arrived within 12 minutes, stabilized Justin's arm and immobilized his leg. Then they took him to the nearest emergency room at Simmons Hospital. Justin was admitted to the hospital and remained there Thursday night, returning to work the following Monday. He is to avoid any heavy type of work; and for a week, according to the doctor, he should work only half a day.

All of the people involved in the report met a week after Justin came back to work to discuss the accident. In addition to the people listed above, the union representative, Kay Thomas, was in attendance. The safety officer of the company, Amy Macfarlane, was also present.

Prepare the report of the accident. Send the report to the CEO, Alice Parsons. Also send a copy to everyone involved in the accident review meeting.

TO: George Clemens, CEO

FROM: Your Name

DATE: Current Date

SUBJECT: Accident of Steve Williams

Introduction

An Accident Review was conducted on September 6, 20xx at 2:00 p.m. in the Conference Room at Clemens Construction, 4987 Main Avenue, Mt. Pleasant, Michigan. The purpose of the meeting was to review the accident of Steve Williams, Director of Marketing and Sales.

Those in attendance at the review were the following:

> Steve Williams, Injured Employee
> Bill Scott, Employee
> Elliot Carson, Employee
> Dale Collins, Union Representative
> Lisa Saunders, Safety Representative
> You, Executive Secretary and Company Business Writer

Accident Summary

Steve Williams, job inspector for Clemens Construction, stopped by a construction job at 39873 Gooding Road, Mt. Pleasant, Michigan, on August 15, 20xx to perform his duties as on-site job inspector. Bill Scott was working there, stringing electrical wire; and Steve was checking with Bill about the materials necessary for rewiring the house, built in 1855. Numerous renovations are being completed by Clemens Construction.

Accident Details and Findings

The following accident details were taken from the accident review meeting held on September 6, 20xx:

Steve climbed a ladder to look at the progress of the wiring. One of the rungs on the ladder, the one immediately below the top rung, gave way under Steve; and he fell to the ground, dislodging his left knee and breaking his right arm in three places.

Bill ran to Steve and put a pillow under his head and to cover him with a blanket. Steve complained about being cold. Bill called Elliot Carson, another employee, to stay with Steve while the EMT team was called.

The EMT arrived at the construction site in about 10 minutes. Emergency medical attention was administered, and Steve was loaded into the ambulance and taken to Riverfront Hospital in Mt. Pleasant.

Steve was in the hospital for four days and will be off work for three to four weeks, according to the doctor.

In addition to the persons who were at the accident scene, the union representative, Dale Collins, and the safety representative, Lisa Saunders, were present at the meeting to discuss the accident.

Corrective Actions

To prevent a recurrence of such an accident happening again, the Safety Department requires the following actions in the future:

1. When working on a ladder, be sure the ladder is safe and is not outdated.

2. All employees working with electrical equipment must wear safety glasses and safety gloves at all times.

3. All employees must consider the possibility of shock for an injured employee. If crew members cannot leave the job site to care for the injured employee, someone on the crew must call 911 for assistance.

4. The company must be notified immediately. The union representative is to be notified within 24 hours.

5. The job site must be closed for the rest of the day. Work cannot begin again until the company and the union are satisfied that good safety practices prevail.

6. The company safety representative will conduct a review of safety procedures within two weeks of the accident. All employees will be expected to attend.

TOPIC	**Progress or Interim Report** (example page 185)
DEFINITION	A progress report is prepared periodically giving the status of a report or a project.
BACKGROUND	If you are working on a project, your supervisor needs to know what has been accomplished to date and what remains to be completed.

KEY POINTS

1. **Introduction**. The introduction to a progress report contains a brief statement of the purpose, overview, background, and nature of the project. Because your supervisor may have many projects going at the same time from many different individuals or teams, he or she will appreciate knowing the exact title and description of the project.

2. **Work completed.** The work completed section provides all pertinent information about the present status of the project, including:

   a. A summary of the work finished during prior reporting periods.
   b. A summary of the work finished since the last report.

3. **Work yet to be completed.** This section is an overview of the remaining work to be done on the project, with target dates. An estimate of the final deadline date appears in this section.

4. **Conclusion.** The concluding section of a progress report is used to bring certain information about the goals of the project to the attention of the person authorizing the work. The conclusion might, for example, explain current or projected delays or cost overruns so that, if necessary, the reader can anticipate or make contingency plans.

STEPS

1. Use memo format to prepare a progress report. Indicate the TO, FROM, DATE, and SUBJECT.

2. Keep the progress report short. Rarely will you have a report more than one page.

3. Send a copy of the progress report to your supervisor and to any one else involved in the writing of the report.

1. Prepare a progress report for a task you are working on in this class or another class.

2. Prepare a progress report in memo format on your status as a student at this university. Write a short introduction; state the work you have completed; tell what has yet to be completed before you graduate from the university, and give the date you expect to graduate.

3. Prepare a progress report for a project you worked on in an internship or in a summer job.

4. Choose one of the classes you are taking this semester. Write a short paper citing your progress so far in the class. Submit the report in a memo to your instructor.

TO: Tom Slick

FROM: Amy Downing, *AD* Mike Feeney, MF Laura Shumaker *LS*

DATE: March 27, 20xx

SUBJECT: Progress Report for Training Session

Introduction: The need for our employees to conduct business abroad has led to the development of a cultural sensitivity training session. We are preparing this training session to improve the knowledge of our employees about other cultures. Our goal is to increase their awareness of business practices and cultural differences in other countries as a result of this training experience. We have developed a time line outlining the major goals and objectives, including the dates we expect to complete each goal or objective.

Work Completed: We have completed a survey of employees to determine their current knowledge related to cultural sensitivity issues. We have developed a preliminary outline of the training session, including the major topics to be included based on the results of our survey. We are also designing activities that will make the training session interactive while reinforcing the information.

Work to be Completed: We are in the process of gathering the materials and resources to include in the training session. The materials and resources should be gathered by April 1. Our next goal is to prepare the necessary promotional material by April 5 to distribute to employees, informing them of the training session.

Anticipated Problems: At this time, we do not anticipate any problems in completing the training session on time. We expect to be prepared to conduct the training session, as planned, on April 15.

TOPIC	**Executive Summary** (examples pages 189-190)

DEFINITION   An executive summary is a condensed report summarizing concisely the contents of a longer document. An executive summary is also used to summarize the contents of an oral presentation.

BACKGROUND   An executive summary serves two functions: (1) the executive summary may be used as a condensed version taking the place of the original document or presentation, or (2) the executive summary may serve to introduce the important features of a longer document that will be read on another occasion.

KEY POINTS

1. Study the original document or presentation carefully. Determine the items you feel are most important and that are representative of the original document.

2. Summarize the contents of the material into a few precise paragraphs that will serve as a reliable summary for another reader. **Avoid stating your opinions or your thoughts**. The paper is a summary, not a critical review.

3. Format the executive summary using block or modified block style. Use memo format for internal distribution.

4. Give a complete citation at the top of the page if you are summarizing written material. Websites provide information on formatting guidelines for the major style guides (such as APA and MLA.) Refer to the website sources listed on the following page.

5. When summarizing an oral presentation, include the name of the speaker(s), the date, and the location of the presentation. If other pertinent information is available, include that information, too.

6. Single-space the paragraphs, but double space between them.

7. Keep the length of an executive summary of written material to about 10 percent of the original length of the written material.

8. Keep the length of an executive summary of an oral presentation short and to the point.

1. Find a two- or three-page article in a current popular news or financial magazine such as *Time, Newsweek, U.S. News and World Report, Fortune* or some other popular business magazine. Prepare an executive summary of the article to turn in with a copy of the original article attached.

2. Write an executive summary for a lecture on campus or a presentation from a guest speaker you heard in a class.

3. Watch a news show or listen to a speaker on the television. Prepare an executive summary of the presentation.

4. Write an executive summary of one of your instructor's classroom presentations. Give your instructor a copy of your summary.

5. Write an executive summary of a non-business article you have read recently. If you have a copy of the article, attach the article to the summary.

6. Write a summary in executive style of a movie or television show you have seen lately. Select two people—one who **has** seen the movie or television show and one who **has not** seen the movie nor the television show—and have them read your summary. Compare the differences in the two summaries. Note the differences in the responses. Decide whether your summary was detailed enough.

7. Read three closely related articles from a popular magazine or newspaper on some topic that may be of interest to you or to others. Write an executive summary combining the three articles into one summary. Include a citation for each of the articles. Hand in the executive summary to your instructor.

8. Give a short presentation of the executive summary you completed in No. 7 to the class. Be prepared to answer questions on the content of your presentation and questions on how you combined the summaries and prepared the report.

http://hbswk.hbs.edu/archive/3660.html- tips from Harvard Business School on creating a powerful executive summary.

www.edc-iitd.org/files/exec_summary.pdf - sample of an executive summary.

ABCD CORPORATION

Interoffice Memorandum

TO: Roberta Johnson, Marketing Manager

FROM: Your Name

DATE: Current Date

SUBJECT: Executive Summary of Article

<u>Article Summarized</u>: Morales, Lourdes. "Great Times at Feather, Inc., All the Time," *Business Weekly News,* January 31, 20xx, pp. 14-17.

Currently, Feather, Inc., located in Mount Pleasant, Michigan, is looking to expand the company's horizons. The Marketing Research Division recently conducted a research study to find whether locating a branch of the company in Germany would be beneficial to the parent company.

Through extensive research, the division reached the conclusion that Germany would not be able to support the current market line due to cultural factors, location of the plant, language barriers, poor climate, high liability, and a bleak outlook for available employees.

Recommendations made to the President and CEO of Feather, Inc., are the following: (1) keep looking for a suitable site in Europe; (2) watch the European economy for any signs of improvement; and (3) consider establishing an additional plant in the southern part of the United States.

GREATTIMES ENTERPRISES, INC.

Interoffice Memorandum

TO: John Jackson, Information Systems Manager

FROM: Your Name

DATE: Current Date

SUBJECT: Executive Summary: Oral Presentation of Joshua Hayes, Public Relations
               Director, Greattimes Enterprises, Inc., November 16, 200x.

Employee benefits are a rapidly growing and an increasingly important form of employee
compensation for both for-profit and nonprofit organizations. According to a
recent U.S. Chamber of Commerce survey, benefits now constitute 47 percent of all
payroll costs, averaging $10,732 yearly for each employee. Thus, based on cost alone,
an organization's benefit program must be carefully monitored and evaluated.

To ensure that the benefit program for Greattimes Enterprises, Inc., is operating as
effectively as possible, the company CEO, Sylvia Bonds, authorized the release of this
information at this presentation, held on November 16, 200x, at Kaiser Auditorium in
Mount Pleasant, Michigan.

A majority of the employees are satisfied with all benefits, although retirement benefits
generated substantial dissatisfaction for each staff employee. In addition, the company
reevaluated the attractiveness of the automobile insurance benefit in one year to
determine staff employees' knowledge about, use of, and desire for this benefit.

Greattimes Enterprises, Inc., must still determine the feasibility of generating an annual
individualized benefit statement for each staff employee.

Greattimes plans a follow-up study of the retirement benefits to determine how
competitive they are with those benefits offered by comparable public and private
business.

TOPIC	**Preparing Written Instructions** (example page 193)

DEFINITION	Instructions are written for the use of products, procedures, practices, and policies.

EXPLANATION	Guidelines for writing instructions are usually included in the company employee manual. Instructions include the basic rules of writing and are divided into three sections: an introduction, a body, and a closing.

KEY POINTS

The introduction. The introduction to any instructions should provide basic information about the product or service or task and should answer the questions, who, what, when, where, why, and how.

1. **The body.** Write the actual directions you want the reader to follow in the order you want those directions followed.

    a. The first word of every numbered instruction should begin with an *active* verb; such as, *gather, place, pull, turn, remove, flip, start, stop, turn, do.*

    b. Finish the instruction with additional sentences; these sentences can use an active or nonactive verb.

    c. Instructions should be understandable by all who read them. Short, concise sentences help readability. Long, complicated words, terms, and phrases that are not easily understood by everyone should be avoided.

    d. Include a warning or caution if needed. Think of ways the users could harm themselves in the use of the product or service.

2. **The closing.** Close with a separate paragraph. Give some encouragement to the reader for following these instructions (*e.g.,* If you follow these instructions, you should have many years of use from your new blender.")

ACTIVITIES

1. Write instructions for one of the following office tasks: (a) how to give CPR in the office; (b) what to do in case of a disaster, such as an earthquake, fire, or explosion; (c) how to fax a document; (d) how to use proper procedures for recycling; or (e) what tips to use for reducing stress.

2. Use the Internet and the library to find a list of "active" verbs Cite the website where you retrieved the information. Send a list of at least 50 active verbs to your instructor in memo format.

3. Write instructions for a task that you select.

4. Write instructions for playing the card game "Fish" or "Crazy Eights" or another card game. Form teams of card players who will follow *exactly* your written instructions. After the game is over, allow each of the team members to offer suggestions as to how the instructions could be written to make them clearer. Each team should rewrite the instructions—then all teams play the game again using their own rewritten rules.

5. Bring a small appliance and a list of instructions that detail the use of that small appliance. Choose someone from the class to read the instructions and use the appliance in front of the rest of the class. Are the instructions easy to follow? What suggestions can the class members make that would make the instructions clearer? Discuss.

6. Write instructions for giving CPR to a person who just fainted in your office or who is choking on a piece of roll.

XYZ CORPORATION

Interoffice Memorandum

TO: All Employees

FROM: Your Name, Human Resources Director

DATE: Current Date

SUBJECT: Instructions for Most Efficient use of Coffee Breaks at XYZ Corp.

Employees are offered two coffee breaks of 15 minutes each—one break in the morning and the other in the afternoon. The following are to serve as guidelines for coffee breaks:

1. **Set a specific time.** Before arriving at work, schedule two break times. Make sure one break is in the morning and the other in the afternoon.

2. **Set your watch to a work clock.** Make sure that your watch reads the same time as your work clock does.

3. **Look at the clock.** Be aware of the time and how long you have until your break starts. **Warning:** If you leave the building, a greater risk occurs that you will not arrive back in time; others may report you for doing so.

4. **Take your break.** When the designated time has arrived, you may leave. As you are leaving, tell a colleague that you are going on break. In this way, you will not be abusing your coffee break.

5. **Look at the clock.** Make sure you look at your clock while you are on break so you know how much time you have left.

6. **Start to work.** When your break is over, you should start working again. Utilize the same process for the afternoon break.

Two coffee breaks are given to each employee twice a day. These privileges can be lost if employees abuse their privileges. Follow the above steps to ensure your freedom and relaxation during working hours.

TOPIC	**Preparing a Press Release** (example page 199)
DEFINITION	A press release, also known as a news release or a media release, is an announcement sent to the media relating something that is taking place in your company that you want everyone to know.
BACKGROUND	A release must be clear and concise and should be written with particular attention to the five w's and the one h: who, what, where, when, why, and how. Write the press release so that the most important item is first, the second most important item second, and so on until the release is finished. This type of writing is called the *Inverted Pyramid Style*. The Inverted Pyramid style of writing provides the essence of the story first and adds details in a descending order of importance.

Also, if a newspaper has limited space for the story, the editor will cut the story *starting from the **bottom** paragraph and working upwards until the story fits the space available.* Limit the document to one or two pages. Be credible—have no typos, no misspelled words, and no factual errors. Some companies suggest a limit of 200 to 300 words.

Mention your company in the release. A journalist who picks up your story logically mentions your company in the release.

Note: Some companies have their own procedures for writing press releases. The plan given in this chapter is just *one* of many that may exist. See the website listings for additional information on press releases. |
| **STEPS** | 1. Use company letterhead paper with wide margins that will permit the editor to write in corrections or additions.

2. Indicate when the material is to be released: "For Immediate Release" or "Release on February 25."

3. Write the headline of your release in bold copy. Keep sentences and paragraphs clear and concise.

4. Provide company information with a name and phone number for the editor so that he or she may call you for clarification or additional material. Give a complete company website address *e.g.,* http://www.yourcompanywebsite.com.

5. Type MORE a double space down from the last line on all pages (except the last) if the release is longer than one page.

6. Type the page number at the top left on the second and |

subsequent pages four times with a hyphen between each number so that attention is called to the page.

7. Type a shortened title or description of what the article is about at the right side of the second and subsequent pages.

8. Type END and double space down from the last line of the article.

ACTIVITIES

1. Prepare a press release for a fictitious company that announces plans for a new building in downtown Mt. Pleasant. The following facts, *in no special order*, should be ranked by you from most important to least important.

   a. new office building in downtown Mt. Pleasant
   b. five stories—every office looks out on the city park
   c. purchased from three local businesspersons: Able Cain, Mabel Virgo, and Consuela Schultz
   d. 16,000 square feet of office space
   e. purchased for $143 million
   f. 50 assigned parking spaces; 100 spaces for visitors
   g. walls and partitions are flexible and can be arranged in a variety of ways
   h. will accommodate company's expanding executive force—due to increase in sales
   i. sales have increased 73 percent in the last decade
   j. three sets of restrooms included on each floor
   k. building is accessible to all—physically challenged, etc.
   l. kitchen and dining area on each floor
   m. a "resting" lounge on each floor—contains books for reading, TV, stereo, reclining chairs; coffee and donuts provided daily
   n. auditorium for conferences and seminars will seat up to 500

   Use the Inverted Pyramid Style of Writing. Remember to put the *most important* item in the first paragraph. Then put the *next most important* item in the next paragraph and so on until the final paragraph contains the *least important* item.
   The reason for this type of writing procedure is that some newspapers will not have space for the entire story you submitted. In order to get the story to fit in the space available, the editor will cut the story, beginning from the bottom paragraph and moving up. So, that is the reason you need to put the most important items at the beginning of the story.

195

The press release is from you, the head of the public relations department, and should be marked for immediate release.

2. Write a press release that announces that YOU are the new sales director for ABCD Corporation. You will start at the beginning of next month. Provide interesting facts and information. Include all the necessary details and write the story in the Inverted Pyramid Style.

3. Write a story about one of your friends who has received the honor of being the first person in his family to complete a college education. Find some interesting facts about the person, and include those facts in the story. The story will be featured in the Sunday edition of the *Morning Sun* as a feature article.

4. Find a press release of a company in one of the local newspapers. Study the article carefully. What do you see as the differences in that article compared to the standards and principles used in this section of the text? Write a memo to your instructor. Attach a copy of the article you found.

5. Write a press release for the local newspaper announcing that your company is now smoke-free. No smoking is permitted within 100 feet of the building.

6. Write a press release announcing that a CMU student has received a $500 award for SAP (a highly regarded software) excellence. John Taylor will be honored at a luncheon at Henegar's Restaurant on April 25, 201-, for outstanding course work performance in his SAP solutions to solve real business problems. Frank Andera, director of CMU's SAP University Alliance Program, said "SAP is an enterprise-wide software solution that links an entire organization together with one computer information system. John Taylor has done an excellent job in his work with SAP." In addition to the $500, Taylor will also receive a certificate, and a plaque with his accomplishment will be held in the SAP Computer Center.

RESOURCES

www.press-release-writing.com – a website devoted to writing press releases; provides ten essential tips on writing effective press releases.

www.publicityinsider.com/ - provides information on publicity secrets for savvy businesses including writing press releases and news releases.

http://service.prweb.com/learning/article/quality-online-press-releases/ - provides information on quality online press releases focused on small businesses; check out the "Related Content" sidebar for additional resources including information on how to write press releases that are search-engine optimization (SEO) friendly and a social media survival kit for small businesses.

Putting the Story Together – Creating a Press Release

Prepare the *lead* (the first part of news story that provides the most important facts of the story in the fewest words possible.) The lead should answer the following questions:

- *Who* was involved?
- *What* happened?
- *When* did it happen?
- *Where* did it happen?
- *Why* did it happen?
- *How* did it happen?

These questions are the ones that the reader wants answered immediately. An effective news story will answer all six questions if they are answerable at the time when the story breaks.

Another requirement of the lead is the *attribution statement,* usually placed at the end of the lead. The attribution tells the reader where the information came from. Note the following example of a lead that utilizes the who, what, when, where, why, and how, along with the attribution statement:

*A young man **(who)** was fatally injured **(what)** Saturday evening **(when)** at the intersection of Maple and Elm streets **(where)** as his car entered the intersection **(how)** as a young boy broke loose from his mother's hand and ran in front of the car, **(why)** according to a police officer. **(attribution statement)**

-Then complete the remainder of the story with the information at your disposal:

John Foster, 28, of 2345 Main Avenue, Mt. Pleasant, died Saturday evening at the corner of Maple and Elm Streets when he swerved to miss Joey Heatherford, the three-year-old son of Josh and Maria Heatherford of 153 North Oak Boulevard. Foster missed the boy, who had run from his mother's grasp. Foster's car skidded into a telephone poll, fatally injuring him. Officers said that Foster was dead instantly at the scene. Joey Heatherford was not injured. Foster, employed at ABCD Corporation since 2001, is survived by his wife of five years, Emily, a daughter, Amelia, 3, and a son, Eric, 18 months. Funeral arrangements are pending.

CMU
Central Michigan University

MEDIA RELATIONS CONTACT: Pat Lawson, 989-555-4654 www.company.edu

CMU CONTACT: Frank Andera, 989-774-6503 www.ander1f@cmich.edu

CMU STUDENTS RECEIVE $500 DOW REWARDS FOR SAP EXCELLENCE

MOUNT PLEASANT – "Three Central Michigan University students with exceptional academic achievements in their study of SAP business software will receive $500 each at a noon luncheon on April 7 at The Embers in Mount Pleasant," according to Dr. Frank Andera, director of CMU's SAP University Alliance Program

Undergraduate students, James Smith of Macomb and James Elias of Clare, and graduate student, Kathleen Parker of Houghton Lake will each receive The Dow/SAP Award of Excellence for their outstanding course work and performance in writing solutions to business problems for SAP applications.

"They are being recognized by The Dow Chemical Company for their outstanding course work performance in their preparation of ABAP/4 Programming solutions to solve real business problems," said Frank Andera, director of CMU's SAP University Alliance Program. "SAP is a market and technology leader in enterprise application software, providing solutions for companies of all sizes and all industry sectors."

- James Smith, Jr., the son of James Smith of Detroit, and Maureen Smith of Macomb, is a graduate of Lakota High School.
- James Elias, the son of Terri Carter of Topeka, Kansas, and George Elias of Grand Rapids, is a graduate of Paw Paw High School. He is a member of the SAP Student Users Group and CMU's Association of Information Technology Professionals student chapter. He served as webmaster and membership chairman last fall.
- Kathleen Parker, the daughter of Sheryl and Brian Parker of Houghton Lake, graduated from Springfield High School in Flint and is a graduate student completing a Master of Science in information systems degree
- CMU's dean of the College of Business Administration, Roland Cole, and CMU President John Robins will speak at the event. Numerous dignitaries from the Dow Chemical Company also will attend the ceremony.
- SAP is an enterprise-wide software solution that links an entire organization together with one computer information system. The German-based company offers software that shares information in real time with employees, suppliers and distributors no matter the size of the organization.

MORE

199

- "SAP software is used by many Michigan companies such as Dow Chemical, Dow Corning, Steelcase, Whirlpool, General Motors, EDS, Ernst & Young, and many others, and CMU's College of Business Administration has been a national leader in integrating its business courses with enterprise resource planning concepts and understandings since 1997," said Andera.

END

TOPIC	**Writing a Proposal** (example page 204)
DEFINITION	A business proposal is a plan of intent to fill a need. Proposals can cover almost any subject and are either **solicited**, submitted in response to a written announcement or request for proposal (RFP), or **unsolicited**, proposals that sell a service or product to an individual or an organization that has not requested a proposal. Proposals tell a person, group, or agency what you will do, when you will do it, and how much it will cost in terms of time and resources.
BACKGROUND	The writer of a proposal tries to show that the proposal, if implemented, will lead to the solving a need or problem for the business. Answer these questions before you begin the proposal:

    a. What is the subject of the proposal?
    b. For whom is the proposal intended?
    c. How do you intend the proposal to be used?
    d. What is the deadline date for submission of the proposal and for tentative implementation of the proposed solution?
    e. Have you reviewed the literature on the Internet and in the library that will provide support for your proposal? How have other companies handled similar situations?

STEPS

1. **Introduce and summarize the background for the proposal.** Who authorized the proposal? Your supervisor? Your department head? The CEO? Identify your readers. Did you come up with the idea on your own? Who is the audience for your proposal? Will your proposal be presented only in writing, or will you be asked to present the proposal orally?

2. **State what you propose to do.** What is the proposal about? What do you want to see happen within the company, within your department, within your office? What is your overall plan?

3. **Provide the scope of the proposal.** What do you plan to include? What will you *not* include? How will you restrict the proposal (delimitations)? What restrictions may occur that are not under your control (limitations)?

4. **Gather the information necessary to complete the proposal.** Do you need to prepare and send out a questionnaire to the other employees to get their opinions? Do you need to visit the library or the Internet to gather any kind of information needed to prepare your proposal?

5. **Prepare a work schedule and project a time limit.** When do you think you will finish the project? Prepare a listing of target dates; for instance, you may wish to break down the time periods into one- or two-week sessions. Your boss may ask you for periodic progress reports until the proposal is finished.

6. **Prepare a list of resources needed**: money, equipment, and additional help? Do you need time away from your job to complete the proposal? What else do you need?

7. **Request approval.** After you have prepared the proposal, ask for approval to go ahead and do what you have proposed to do.

ACTIVITIES

1. Using one of the following situations, prepare an organizational proposal. Use the material you just read to prepare the proposal. You may assume that you have been asked to prepare a proposal (solicited) or that you have come up with an idea of your own (unsolicited.) See the sample proposal at the end of this section.
   a. a drug testing and drug awareness program for your company
   b. a childcare program for all employees
   c. three new PC's for your department
   d. an up-to-date web page for your employees
   e. in-house training program for all employees regarding any one of the following workplace issues:
      - sexual harassment
      - attendance at company-sponsored events
      - a no-smoking policy within the building
      - a day-care facility for all employees
   f. a speaker's series where outstanding leaders in business are invited to speak to all employees.

2. Prepare a second proposal. Use one of the ideas mentioned in Activity 1 above; or, come up with an original idea that will get the approval of your instructor.

3. Search the Internet or go to the library to see what other information you can find about *internal* and *external* proposals. Also, read more about *solicited proposals, unsolicited proposals,* and *RFP (request for proposal).* Send your instructor a short memo of your findings.

4. Identify the following proposal terms: investigative proposal, organizational proposal, and product proposal. Prepare a short memo of your findings for your instructor.

5. Investigate two of the website sources listed below. Prepare and submit to your instructor a short memo summarizing the websites.

RESOURCES

www.learnerassociates.net/proposal - guide for writing a funding proposal.

www.theresearchassistant.com – a comprehensive source of tips and tools for the steps for preparing and writing a proposal.

http://foundationcenter.org/getstarted/tutorials/shortcourse/index.html - a proposal writing short course with step-by-step instructions and explanations.

WXYZ Corporation

Interoffice Memorandum

TO: Claudia L. Finch, Supervisor, Projects Department

FROM: Alonzo Evening, Project Director $\mathcal{AE}$
                 Jason Bach, Assistant Project Director $\mathcal{SB}$

DATE: October 15, 20xx

SUBJECT: Proposal for Globalization Options

Attached is a proposal for globalization options for WXYZ Corporation. Our team has researched the topic and feels that we can conduct the study for our company. The following information will help you determine whether or not completing the study is feasible.

The Project

WXYZ is interested in expanding its operations—either in this country or overseas. Currently, the division feels that Switzerland would be a compatible international market place for products from our company. Therefore, a study of the culture and the economy of Switzerland to determine if that country is a viable option for this move will be undertaken.

Authorization and Background

Earlier this month, you mentioned that our company was exploring globalization options and that those employees who wanted to take part in presenting a proposal are asked to do so. We as project directors of the company want to take part in the project. This proposal is submitted in response to your request.

<u>Purpose</u>

The purpose is to investigate, through both primary and secondary research, the feasibility of Switzerland as an international outlet for WXYZ Corporation. A further purpose of this proposal is to make information available to WXYZ management information and facts for expanding or not expanding into Switzerland.

Scope

To determine if WXYZ Corporation should take steps to locate an international outlet within the borders of Switzerland, the following questions must be answered:

1. Would the Swiss culture be open to an American toy manufacturer producing products in Switzerland?

2. Is the Swiss economy strong enough to support a recreational products manufacturer?

3. Would our products be acceptable in their culture?

4. What are the cultural norms of Switzerland pertaining to business socialization?

Delimitations

The study will be confined to research conducted on the Swiss culture. This research will be conducted using library information, Internet sources, and personal contact with members of that culture.

Limitations

The sources obtained may not adequately convey how the culture realistically functions as a whole. Depending on which part of the country the sources are gathered, different viewpoints may exist. Therefore, the views and opinions should serve as a preliminary guideline to determine if further research should be conducted of other sectors of the population.

Methodology

Data Collection. Primary data will be obtained through research conducted electronically as well as personal interviews with knowledgeable persons. Each project director of each team will be responsible for collecting the data. Secondary sources from the library and from the Internet will be used whenever feasible.

Data Analysis. These data will be used to determine whether a move to Switzerland will be appropriate at this time. The information will be evaluated on a subjective basis.

<u>Data Presentation</u>. The project directors will submit the findings, conclusions, and recommendations to the supervisor of the project. In addition, the supervisor will receive a progress report approximately every two weeks. The final report will be compiled into a presentation format, which will be presented to employees of WXYZ Corporation during the early part of December.

Project Time Line

Since the project directors have other responsibilities while working on this project, approximately three weeks will be needed to complete the study. The estimated time to complete the entire project is 40 hours. The following is a schedule of targeted dates:

Conduct research	November 1, 200x
Analyze data	November 15, 200x
Complete the report	November 20, 200x
Presentation of findings	December 1, 200x

Resources Needed

The project directors will use an average of 20 hours to conduct the research and 20 hours to analyze and interpret the data. The cost of supplies is due to long-distance charges stemming from international communication with Swiss residents and officials. The remaining time will be devoted to determining the best way to present the data to the employees. Currently, a written report and a PowerPoint presentation are anticipated. Total estimated cost is $24,500.

Additional help	$6,000
Phone expenses	5,000
Miscellaneous	4,500
Travel	9,000
Total Estimated Cost	$24,500

Request for Approval

Your approval of this proposal by October 25, 20xx, will permit the project to begin and end according to the above schedule. If you have any questions regarding the proposal, please call or email either or both of us. Your reply is eagerly anticipated.

TOPIC	**Preparing a Code of Ethics** (example page 210)
DEFINITION	A code of ethics sets the ethical climate for an organization. A code of ethics sets a standard for correct and honest behavior and tells how ethical issues will be handled within the organization. A code of ethics must identify the main responsibilities and commitments to all of the organization's constituencies and to the public.
BACKGROUND	Management must encourage ethical awareness in their organizations from the top to the bottom. Many companies provide training programs to increase sensitivity to ethical issues. Ethical codes of conduct must maintain a strong and ethical climate; help to create an appealing work environment; and increase employee loyalty, morale, and motivation. All ethical codes must enhance the public's image of the organization.
KEY POINTS	

Qualities of ethical behavior in business consist of the following characteristics or traits:

1. **Honesty and Integrity.** Employees must be truthful, frank, and sincere.

2. **Trustworthiness.** Employees must keep promises and fulfill commitments.

3. **Loyalty.** Employees must be devoted to their tasks and be true to persons and institutions.

4. **Fairness.** Equal treatment to all employees must prevail.

5. **Caring.** Concern for the well being of others is necessary. Kindness is required.

6. **Respect.** Employees must be courteous and considerate and respect the dignity and privacy of others.

7. **Responsibility.** Employees must be competent to carry out their duties in the best interest of others.

8. **Accountability.** Employees must accept responsibility for their consequences, actions, and decisions in the pursuit of

1. After an ethical audit by an ad hoc committee of your
    company, Smith and Brothers, the company was found to be in
    violation of its ethical code. According to the audit, not all
    ethical areas were covered by the current code. According to
    the audit, the following areas must be covered in any code of
    ethics:

    a. Safety for products, services, and people
    b. Equal opportunity for employment
    c. Compliance with laws and regulations
    d. Sexual harassment
    e. Personal relationships
    f. Giving of gifts
    g. Private employment outside the company and other
        conflicting roles
    h. Endorsements

    Use the Internet, an annual report, or personal visits to
    companies to find examples of codes of ethics. Refer to the
    sample code of ethics. Write a one-page code of ethics for
    your classroom.

2. Conduct an ethical compliance audit by visiting a company in
    your area. Ask the following questions and any others you
    think necessary to find out about the company's code of ethics.
    Prepare a memo to your instructor with your results.

    a. Does the company have a code of ethics?
    b. Who is responsible for seeing the code is enforced?
    c. What happens to people who do not obey the code?
    d. Is the code of ethics made public? Has the code
        appeared in the newspaper? Is the code made available
        to all employees of the company?
    e. Is the code listed in the company manual?
    f. How does top management detect the ethical issues that
        need to be resolved?
    g. How do employees report unethical conduct?
    h. Is the code of ethics under constant scrutiny to see that
        all areas are covered?
    i. Does your company have an ethics committee?
    j. Is there consistent enforcement of standards and
        punishments in the organization?
    k. Is the code of ethics updated periodically?

3. Using the Internet and the library, search for information
    about the Federal Sentencing Guidelines. What do these
    guidelines have to do with codes of ethics? What influence

do these guidelines have on codes of ethics? Write a short memo to your instructor that summarizes the Federal Sentencing Guidelines and how these guidelines can be used to structure a Code of Ethics for your company.

4. Join in a class discussion with the other class members as to whether or not they have ever worked in a company that has a code of ethics. What were their reactions to working under such a code? Do the workers feel that the code of ethics worked? What were some problems with the code?

5. Have you ever worked at a company that did not have a Code of Ethics? Perhaps the company did have a Code of Ethics and you were not aware of it? How can you find out about the ethical climate at a company in which you work? Discuss.

6. Discuss in a team situation what diversity issues you might need to consider in developing a Code of Ethics? Present your findings orally to the other class members.

RESOURCES

www.studentcenter.ja.org/aspx/LearnEthics - defines ethics as rules; gives illustrations of ethical businesses.

www.ethics.org – provides information on ethical practices in business.

www.ethicsweb.ca/codes - provides instructions on how to write a code of ethics including information for implementation and enforcement of codes of ethics.

CODE OF ETHICS

The Old Frontier Corporation
(Revised January 15, 20xx)

The Old Frontier Corporation is committed to treating our employees, our customers, and our suppliers with honesty, integrity, trustworthiness, fairness, respect, reliability, and safety.

Honesty and sincerity; truthfulness
Unquestionable integrity
Ability to keep promises; trustworthiness
Respect for all people
Reliability; always seeking excellence
Safety in the workplace

Guiding Principles

1. The Old Frontier Corporation will obey all laws, rules, and regulations.

2. Products and services will be consistent with quality and safety standards.

3. The Old Frontier Corporation supports and encourages diversity in the workplace. No one will be discriminated against because of race, color, religion, gender, national origin, political affiliation, physical handicap, age, marital status, or sexual orientation.

4. Customer satisfaction with products and services will be a top concern.

5. The Old Frontier Corporation will review and adapt to changing consumer needs all trends in the marketplace.

The Code of Ethics of The Old Frontier Corporation is designed to establish and maintain a pleasant, safe, and ethical climate in which to work in order to maintain the public's positive image of our company.

TOPIC   **Evaluating Website Content**

KEY POINTS

1. Finding quality information on the Internet requires analysis and critical thinking skills.

2. Written resources found on the Internet must be critically evaluated to determine the quality of the information—all websites are not created equal.

3. The five most basic criteria to base your evaluation of websites include:
    a. Accuracy
    b. Authenticity
    c. Objectivity
    d. Currency
    e. Coverage

4. Evaluating the content of websites involves the analysis of a number of issues related to these five basic criteria, such as:
    a. Is the information dated?
    b. What is the expertise of the author?
    c. Is the information objective?
    d. Is the purpose of the site stated?
    e. Is adequate information provided regarding how
    f. research was conducted, data gathered, etc.?
    g. Are sources cited as to where/how the information was
    h. retrieved?

5. Understanding "who" the author or publisher of a web page is also important. By looking at the address (URL) of the website you can determine the domain:
    a. Education site – *.edu* in the address
    b. Government site - *.gov* in the address
    c. Commercial site - *.com* in the address
    d. Network site - *.net* in the address

    Be aware that within any given domain there is a wide range of quality. Just because a website has, for example, an education domain does not guarantee the accuracy or quality of the information. You can look up domain name extensions and what they mean on websites like www.quackit.com/domain-names/domain_name_extension_definitions.cfm.

Five Criteria for Evaluating Web Pages

Source: http://olinuris.library.cornell.edu/ref/research/webcrit.html

Evaluation of Web Documents

1. *Accuracy of Web Documents*

   - Who wrote the page and can you contact him or her?
   - What is the purpose of the document and why was it produced?
   - Is this person qualified to write this document?

2. *Authority of Web Documents*

   - Who published the document, and is it separate from the "Webmaster"?
   - Check the domain of the document, what institution publishes this document?
   - Does the publisher list his or her qualifications?

3. *Objectivity of Web Documents*

   - What goals/objectives does this page meet?
   - How detailed is the information?
   - What opinions (if any) are expressed by the author?

4. *Currency of Web Documents*

   - When was it produced?
   - When was it updated?
   - How up-to-date are the links (if any)?

5. *Coverage of the Web Documents*

   - Are the links (if any) evaluated and do they complement the documents' theme?
   - Is it all images or a balance of text and images?
   - Is the information presented cited correctly?

How to Determine the Basics

Accuracy
- Make sure author provides email or a contact address/phone number.
- Know the distinction between author and Webmaster.

Authority
- What credentials are listed for the author?
- Where is the document published? Check URL domain.

Objectivity

- Determine if page is a mask for advertising; if so, information might be biased.
- View any Web page as you would an infomercial on television; ask why was this written/for whom?

Currency

- How many dead links are there?
- Are the links current or updated regularly?
- Is the information outdated?

Coverage

- If page requires special software to view, how much are you missing if you don't have the software?
- Is it free or is there a fee for info?
- Is there an option for text only, or frames, or a suggested browser for better viewing?

From *C RL News,* July/August 1998: 522-523, "Teaching undergrads WEB evaluation: A guide for library instruction" by Jim Kapoun. Copyright 1998 by Jim Kapoun. Reprinted by permission of the author.

ACTIVITIES

1. Develop your skills for conducting Internet research and evaluating website content with an *Internet Scavenger Hunt.* Your instructor will provide you with a list of five items for the scavenger hunt. Here are the guidelines:

   a. You must find an exact match for each item listed in the scavenger hunt.

   b. Read the explanation for each item carefully.

   c. You must provide a hard copy print out of the relevant page.

   d. You must provide the exact address (URL) of the source and know who sponsored that source.

   e. You must find all five items to complete the scavenger hunt.

   f. You must turn your sources/printouts into the instructor in person (instructor will record the time and date.)

   g. First person to find all of the items wins!

RESOURCES

www.andyspinks.com/researchhelp/web/CARS.pdf - the CARS checklist for evaluating Internet sources

www.virtualsalt.com/evalu8it.htm - a more detailed checklist on using the CARS checklist.

http://olinuris.library.cornell.edu/ref/research/webeval.html - provides criteria and tools for evaluating websites.

www.studygs.net/evaluate.htm - gives training and strategies for evaluating website content.